Noam Chomsky

A Philosophic Overview

By JUSTIN LEIBER

Herbert H. Lehman College
The City University of New York

ST. MARTIN'S PRESS   NEW YORK

410.924
L53n
101090
May 1977

Cover photo by Christopher S. Johnson

2 3 4 5 6 7 8 9 10 11 12 13 14 15   88 87 86 85 84 83 82 81 80 79 78 77 76

About the Author

Justin Leiber has been assistant professor of philosophy at Lehman College of the City University of New York since 1968. He received his B.A. degree and his Ph.D. from the University of Chicago and holds a graduate degree from the University of Oxford. He has been a visiting teacher at the University of Oxford and the University of London. Dr. Leiber's publications include *Modals and Modalities* and contributions to *Analysis, Review of Metaphysics, University Review,* and other periodicals. His father, Fritz Leiber, is a well-known science fiction writer, whose first novel, *Conjure Wife,* was originally published by Twayne Publishers, Inc. some twenty years ago.

Preface

This is a philosopher's exposition and interpretation of Noam Chomsky's thought, not his life. It would be impertinent to write a personal biography of a man in his early forties, particularly of an individual like Chomsky whose intellectual biography comes close to being a sketch of what has happened to theoretical linguistics and psycholinguistics in the past fifteen years. Besides, as perhaps the only scientist, or philosopher, whose name appears on the Nixon White House enemies list, Chomsky may need no introduction.

Noam Chomsky is one of the most helpful, earnest, charming, and unaffected people I have met. But though I have corresponded and talked with him, he did not see the manuscript of this book until after it had been delivered to the publisher, and this had been my wish. If I had known that he would see the book before publication, I would have felt constrained to write a different sort of book—one which I did not want to write.

This book derives from lectures in a course I gave on Chomsky and Philosophy at Lehman College of the City University of New York in the 1973 spring term. I want to acknowledge the help given me by the students and staff of the college, particularly John Gullo, Sarah Nicholas, Mel Nutovich, and Marty Schatz, and by my colleagues. I want also to express my gratefulness for discussions about linguistics and logic that I had while at Oxford University during the previous two academic years: particularly, to Professor A. J. Ayer, L. A. Dunmore, S. N. Hampshire, H. R. Harré, Dr. Roy Harris, S. C. Martens, Geoffrey Sampson, John Schumacher, and, above all, L. J. Cohen. Thanks, for other reasons, to M. A. E. Dummett, Tom Knight, and Susie A——m, a charming four-year-old transformational-generative device.

Justin Leiber

Herbert H. Lehman College
The City University of New York

SYNTAX is the study of the principles and processes by which sentences are constructed in particular languages. Syntactic investigation of a given language has as its goal the construction of a grammar that can be viewed as a device of some sort for producing the sentences of the language under analysis. More generally, linguists must be concerned with the problem of determining the fundamental underlying properties of successful grammars. The ultimate outcome of these investigations should be a theory of linguistic structure in which the descriptive devices utilized in particular grammars are presented and studied abstractly, with no specific reference to particular languages. One function of this theory is to provide a general method for selecting a grammar for each language, given a corpus of sentences of this language. (Chomsky, *Syntactic Structures*, 1957, p. 11)

The real problem is that of developing a hypothesis about [the] initial structure [of the human mind] that is sufficiently rich to account for the acquisition of language, yet not so rich as to be inconsistent with the known diversity of language. It is a matter of no concern and of only historical interest that such a hypothesis will evidently not satisfy the preconceptions about learning that derive from centuries of empiricist doctrine. These preconceptions are not only quite implausible, to begin with, but are without factual support and are hardly consistent with what little is known about how animals or humans construct a "theory of the external world."

It is clear why the view that all knowledge derives solely from the senses by elementary operations of association and "generalization" should have had much appeal in the context of eighteenth-century struggles for scientific naturalism. However, there is surely no reason today for taking seriously a position that attributes a complex human achievement entirely to months (or at most years) of experience, rather than to millions of years of evolution or to principles of neural organization that may be even more deeply grounded in physical law—a position that would, furthermore, yield the conclusion that man is, apparently, unique among animals in the way in which he acquires knowledge. Such a position is particularly implausible with regard to language, an aspect of the child's world that is a human creation and would naturally be expected to reflect intrinsic human capacity in its internal organization. (Chomsky, *Aspects of the Theory of Syntax*, 1965, p. 58)

A vision of a future social order is in turn based on a concept of human nature. If, in fact, man is an indefinitely malleable, completely plastic being, with no innate structures of mind and no intrinsic needs for a cultural or social character, then he is a fit subject for the "shaping of behavior" by the State authority, the corporate manager, the technocrat, or the central committee. Those with some confidence in the human species will hope this is not so and will try to determine the intrinsic human characteristics that provide the framework for intellectual development, the growth of moral consciousness, cultural achievement, and participation in a free community. In a partly analogous way, a classical tradition spoke of artistic genius acting within and in some ways challenging a framework of rule. Here we touch on matters that are little understood. It seems to me that we must break away, sharply and radically, from much of modern social and behavioral science if we are to move towards a deeper understanding of these matters. (Chomsky, "Language and Freedom," *Abraxas*, 1970, p. 22)

Acknowledgments

The author would like to thank the following publishers: Mouton & Co., The Hague, Netherlands, for permission to quote the first paragraph of *Syntactic Structures*, and for permission to quote the last paragraph on page 198 of *Studies on Semantics in Generative Grammar*; MIT Press for permission to quote from pages 58–59 of *Aspects of the Theory of Syntax*; Scribners & Sons for permission to quote the last sentence on page seven of *The Wind in the Willows* (1960); Random House for permission to quote the first seventy words of William Faulkner's *Requiem for a Nun*, and for permission to quote the last sentence on page 41 and the first on page 42 of *Problems of Freedom and Knowledge*. All rights reserved.

Contents

Introduction

This book is an elementary, self-contained, general, and philosophic introduction to the thought of Noam Chomsky. It is *elementary* in that I have avoided talking about Chomsky's *more* complicated and technical contributions to the mathematical theory of grammars, to syntactical and phonological theory, and to the syntactical and phonological description of the English language.

It is *self-contained* in that I have tried very hard to address myself to the general reader or college student who has no training in linguistics. Hence I spend some time explaining the problems, concepts, and terminology of linguistics and of the mathematical theory of formalized languages, for the reader must know something about these matters if he is to understand Chomsky's own work. Anyone who writes a book of this sort has to decide how far he will go in boring and annoying those readers who already have some relevant background. One must certainly go some distance in this direction for the sake of the reader who has no knowledge of the field. I have gone very far.

This book is a *general* introduction to Chomsky's thought in that I devote a large portion of it to the implications of Chomsky's work for psychology, philosophy, and politics, and to what he has said explicitly about these matters. One of the most striking features of Chomsky's thought is that he wants to break down the recently erected professional borderlines between psychology, philosophy, politics, and linguistics, that is, the divisions between our various sorts of knowledge of the world, man, and language and those between our knowledge of man and our participation in humanity. Certainly, it is what Chomsky has to say about these broader subjects rather than simply about syntax and phonology in the narrow sense that has led to an interest in his work by intellectuals, scholars, and scientists generally. Indeed, it is the broader aspects of Chomsky's ideas that have

13

led some to feel that he may have created one of the few great intellectual revolutions of this century. What I am trying to do here is simply to sketch the developments that have led some people to talk of such an intellectual revolution, rather than attempting to introduce the reader to linguistics, or Chomskyan linguistics, in a narrow sense.

I also stress that this is a *philosophic* introduction to Chomsky's work. This is so in a double sense. My own training and interests make it proper for me to be primarily concerned with the philosophic implications of Chomsky's work. But, also, Chomsky himself has insisted that his work is philosophic in itself, and I want to pay particular attention to this aspect of his thinking, since linguists who write about him do not say much about this.

Chomsky has come to believe that his own work reestablishes and gives commanding support to *rationalism,* a view maintained by many seventeenth- and eighteenth-century philosophers and contrasted with the *empiricism* maintained by other philosophers of the same period. Of course, and this is an important point, these seventeenth- and eighteenth-century philosophers did not think of themselves as philosophers *as opposed to* scientists. Nor did they believe that the dispute between rationalism and empiricism was a philosophic issue *as opposed to* an issue belonging to natural science, psychology, or linguistics. On the whole Chomsky would agree with this traditional view. He believes, that is, that linguistic and psychological research can produce evidence that may tell in favor of rationalism or empiricism. And he believes that his own work has confirmed rationalism.

This claim of Chomsky's has made for some very confused and very emotional debate. This is so because, in this century, most philosophers, psychologists, and scientists generally have taken it for granted that rationalism is as outmoded as alchemy, the divine right of kings, or the view that the world is supported by a giant standing on a tortoise. Equally, philosophers and psychologists have often written as if the apparent victory of empiricism over rationalism were really nothing more than the triumph of truth, objectivity, and science over the forces of superstition, nonsense, and religious and political authoritarianism.

Chomsky does not believe by any means that his work confirms *all* the views associated with rationalism. His political thought and action is anarchist and socialist; and, so I shall argue toward the end of this book, his views are democratic in a way that has been very unfashionable in scholarly thought in this century.

But Chomsky does believe that recent linguistic research has supported three views associated with rationalism: that there is *universal grammar,* that there are *innate ideas,* and that psychology must make use of many *mentalistic* notions. The first view amounts to the claim that, beneath the observed and superficial diversity in the natural languages that men know, there is substantial universality in linguistic categories, rules, and processes. The second view insists that a good portion of this universality is properly explained by assuming that we have *built into us* quite specific and complex techniques and forms for grasping what our environment gives to us through our senses. Mentalism, finally, is the view that psychology, particularly when describing human linguistic activity and thought, must talk in terms of structures and processes that can be tied to observed physical behavior *only* in a very indirect way.

Empiricists, on the other hand, have tended to see each human language as essentially unique, though there may be some essentially accidental similarities between some languages in grammatical categories and rules. They have thought that what we know can be explained by assuming that our environmental experience only needs the assistance of some very simple, and general innate learning techniques (ones which we share with animals). Finally, empiricists have believed that psychology should only deal with observables. In this century, under the label *behaviorism,* this view has almost amounted to the claim that psychology is only concerned with the observed physical behavior of laboratory subjects.

Chomsky's revival of rationalism has led to particularly confusing reactions on the part of philosophers who distinguish philosophy from science, and from psychology in particular. Such philosophers have felt that rationalism was wrong and empiricism right, on purely logical, or narrowly philosophic, grounds (whatever the results of actual scientific theory, observation, and experiment). Consequently, such philosophers have accepted Chomsky's specific results and speculations about innate learning devices but have denied that any such results could ever shake philosophic (or logical) empiricism. They have claimed that Chomsky's work *cannot* justify rationalism because there is, in their view, absolutely *no* alternative to empiricism. No results of actual scientific investigation could ever conflict with "empiricism" according to this view. I shall have more to say about this debate later. But one point that might be made here is that Chomsky's view of the rationalist-empiricist controversy is certainly closer to what the seventeenth- and eighteenth-century parties to that dispute thought they were talking about than his critics generally believe.

The simplest summary I can make of the development of Chomsky's thought follows. He started by asking quite narrow questions about the logical structure of linguists' descriptions of human languages, that is, he began by asking what kinds of rules should appear in a good description of the grammar of a language. But Chomsky found, again and again, that the answers he discovered to these specific formal questions led him to broaden the scope and depth of linguistic study and to support, at a more and more general level, a rationalist view about man and language. New techniques in mathematical logic and the abstract theory of thinking machines, plus his own work, allowed Chomsky to ask precise and formal questions about linguistics and language. His results led him to criticize and discard the prevailing views in linguistics. And he found that his work gave a new and precise justification for more traditional and rationalist views about language and linguistics. Precisely those views, in many cases, that had been condemned as unscientific and nonempirical by the "scientific," or structural, linguistics that Chomsky first learned as a student of Professor Zellig Harris at the University of Pennsylvania just after World War II.

In this introduction to his work, I am going to lay out Chomsky's thought in roughly the same sequence in which it actually developed. I start with the specific inquiry, apparatus, and symbolism that appears in his first book, *Syntactic Structures*, and is significantly developed in *Aspects of the Theory of Syntax* and other works. In the latter portion of this book, I return to the more general philosophic and psychological issues I have just mentioned. But this procedure raises a problem.

Often, in introductions of this sort, the author will spend half of his work talking in very general and philosophic terms about a man's thought, getting to the man's specific claims, technical apparatus, and symbolism only toward the end of the work—as if these were *just* the application of the general ideas of the first half. This way of writing has an advantage. The reader starts with general issues that he knows something about and can see the point of discussing. Indeed, at times the "general issues" almost seem to be put forward as bait which will lead the reader on to the specifics of the technical apparatus. Often this practice has an unasked-for effect: the reader stops (or at least stops paying attention) when the general exposition does, convinced that he has the big picture and can skip the details. But there is a more basic problem with this manner of exposition: in some cases, and most certainly in this case, *one only really understands the generalizations if one sees them as labels for results obtained in the technical apparatus.* Until one has some grasp of the specifics of Chomsky's work one does not really know what he means by rationalism, universal grammar, innate ideas, or mentalism.

It is often remarked that a good symbolism, that is, a good technical apparatus, is a good teacher. This is true both of how Chomsky's thought actually developed and also of the best manner for coming to understand his thought. Hence I shall begin in just this way and return to generalities later on (except for a few remarks about linguistics at the beginning of the next chapter). There is a difficulty in this procedure which we should face now: the reader may not at first see the point, for psychology and philosophy, of talk about kinds of grammars and kinds of grammatical rules. All I can do now for such a reader is promise that he will come to see the point in later sections and ask him to bear with me that far.

What happened when Chomsky confronted the linguistics of his time with various precise questions has a dramatic quality similar to the Michelson-Morley experiment, and a few others, that led to Einstein's relativity theory. In both cases, deep seated preconceptions exploded—in a shocking and baffling way—when attempts were made to work out their implications in new and precise ways. Of course, there are critics who are much less impressed. Perhaps now is an appropriate time to mention a few examples of genuine and not so genuine *scientific revolutions* that have nothing to do with linguistics, so that we will have a stock of examples hovering in the background with which to compare what Chomsky and his associates have done. If we want to know whether what is now going on in linguistics and psycholinguistics really looks like a genuine scientific revolution, we ought to know what a genuine scientific revolution tends to look like. So I will end this introduction by making a few points about Einstein's revolution, and by still more briefly mentioning the theory that the material things in our world are made of atoms, which is a genuine scientific theory if not a revolutionary one, and by offering Freud's theory of the unconscious as a less than fully genuine scientific theory.

The Michelson-Morley experiment attempted to confirm what nineteenth-century physics *seemed to make inevitable*. Familiarly, nineteenth-century physicists were convinced that light consisted of waves. Operating under the preconception that what behaved like a wave could not possibly behave like a particle, these scientists believed that light must be a vibration in some medium, the so-called ether. And given what they knew about wave motion, these scientists inevitably concluded that the speed of light ought to be affected by the drift of the ether, relative to the earth's rotation. Light should move faster or slower depending on whether it was moving with, or against, the ether drift. A very precise attempt was made by Michelson and Morley to measure the extent of the ether-drift effect, and they discovered that the drift effect did not occur at all. Though attempts were made to repair the damage, in a very short period of time some basic preconceptions of nineteenth-century physics were cast aside. Unthinkable possibilities became thinkable. Light could behave like a wave *without* needing a medium and the notion of ether, with all the difficulties it caused, could be dropped. Einstein's work tied together this result with others that ran against the deepest preconceptions of nineteenth-century physics. The position, size, and movement of objects were not, as the previous physics assumed, determined for all observers alike in an absolute space and time; rather, position, size, and movement were determined differently, relative to the viewpoints of various observers. But the difference between the old and the new physics only made a difference in terms of *actual observations* in cases requiring delicate and difficult observational technique: in particular, in those cases where some objects were moving close to the speed of light relative to the observer. Einstein's theory of relativity placed the observational results and low-level generalizations of Newtonian and nineteenth-century physics within a richer conception of physical reality that explained not only these generalizations and results but also the newer results that made the older physics inadequate.

Very roughly, one might think of Chomsky's initial effort at putting the entrenched structuralist linguistic theory in a more precise and formal way as a sort of Michelson-Morley experiment, one which showed in a startling way what was inadequate about structuralist linguistics and about the preconceptions about psychology and philosophy that went with it. Similarly, the subsequent theory of language that Chomsky developed explained many features of language that were beyond structuralist linguistics and placed the specific data, and many lower-level generalizations, of the structuralists within a richer theory. We shall return to this comparison at various stages of the exposition. Right now I am going to list seven points about Einstein's scientific revolution that will be relevant.

1. Some of the deepest preconceptions of the older scientific view lead inevitably, when put precisely and given new techniques of testing, to specific claims, and these claims, quite startlingly, turn out false in *crucial tests*.

2. The older view is contradicted (*observationally*) only when very delicate, precise, unusual, or difficult observations are made. The older view is not false observationally with respect to what could be learned through traditional experiments, through our senses in everyday life, or through commonly available instrumentation.

3. The new view differs from the old in terms of many *very general* claims about reality and about the underlying features

of reality, and it differs in terms of the general explanations that it provides of observed phenomena. Though the new view differs drastically from the old in terms of general theory, of explanation, or of what underlies observation or lies at the threshold of possible observation, it is very similar to the old view in gross observational terms. It is not a scientific revolution just to start making careful observations: revolution comes when *the general* theory of what underlies a mass of established observational data *is shattered by a small amount of data and a lot of theorizing,* and it is replaced by a new general theory of what underlies the original mass of established data plus some new additions.

4. The new view is not automatically accepted, because it challenges deep preconceptions and because the new data are slender and can be explained to some degree by making some new assumptions. The fact that the new assumptions do not seem to be a natural extension of the old view, but rather a clumsy and artificial addition, is a sign that one is seeing a genuine scientific revolution. Another sign is that the new view explains various data that the older view did not or could not explain.

5. The new view is thought to have all sorts of implications of a general and philosophic sort about the nature of scientific inquiry, about reality and man's place in it, and so on. The accusation will be made, sometimes fairly, that the new view is being stretched far beyond its proper sphere of application. When Adolph Hitler attacked Einstein's theory of relativity, it was not because he had strong convictions about the ether or the speed of light. Rather, Hitler was sensitive to the implications of a generalization that both admirers and detractors of Einstein saw as basic to his theory, namely, that the character of reality is *relative* to the viewpoints of various observers and has no absolute character in and of itself. (Chomsky's detractors often suggest that he has turned some narrow but worthwhile contributions to linguistics into wild, sweeping, and mystical claims about language, psychology, and philosophy.)

These five points apply to perhaps anything that could be called a "scientific revolution," but two further points apply more narrowly to Einstein's theory and (I think) to Chomsky's theory.

6. The new view is supported by the availability of a new technical apparatus, or, more precisely, a new formal system that makes the old view (and the formal system that it takes for granted) seem to be making a very *arbitrary* or *special* assumption about reality. The old physics had taken Euclidean geometry for granted. In particular, it accepted the "parallel postulate" that through a point not lying on a given line one and only one line could be drawn parallel to the original line. However, without any thought of practical application, some nineteenth-century mathematicians made the startling discovery that one could have sound, "non-Euclidean" geometries in which no lines, some particular number, or an infinite number, could be drawn parallel to a given line. The availability of these formal systems (Einstein adopted the one in which no lines could be drawn parallel) helped Einstein to argue that the Euclidean geometry which the old physics had taken for granted was really an arbitrary, or special, assumption that did work for the mass of familiar observations but which did not necessarily (and in fact did not) apply to observations that went beyond the normal run of human experience. Similarly, as we shall soon see, Chomsky has shown that the formal system that structuralist linguistics might be said to have taken for granted can be seen to be a special, or arbitrary, case, and one which can be accounted for within a richer formal system.

7. Both Einstein and Chomsky took the step of adding the observer to the data that is to be explained, though in somewhat different ways. Einstein wanted to say that one could not adequately describe things in absolute spatial and temporal terms, but, rather, that one had to describe things in terms of various systems of observation. For example, an object might appear ten feet long relative to an observer whose speed relative to the object is much less than the speed of light, while it might appear eight feet long for an observer moving, relative to the object, at close to the speed of light. Similarly, Chomsky claims that sentences and other linguistic items cannot be fully characterized in terms that do not bring in human beings and their methods of generating and grasping such items. Hence

Chomsky sees linguistics as a branch of psychology in a way that the structuralist linguistics do not.

Notice that the difficulty about whether or not Chomsky's specific results really support philosophical rationalism now reappears as a general characteristic of scientific revolutions. During "nonrevolutionary" periods in science, when scientists work smoothly without questioning various preconceptions, it is probably easier to believe that there is a sharp distinction between specifically scientific and philosophic questions. Certainly, it seems characteristic of scientific revolutions that they call into question distinctions of this sort, that is, that they raise serious questions about the proper *boundaries* of science, about its goals, methods, proper subject matter, and so on.

Two scientific theories have been compared to Chomsky's work by other writers. J. J. Katz, in a book appropriately titled *The Underlying Reality of Language,* suggests that Chomsky's insistence on explaining the superficial diversity of language in terms of universal, underlying psychological realities is like the attempt, first made by the ancient Greek philosopher Democritus, to explain the superficial diversity of chemical mixtures in terms of a relatively small number of kinds of atoms that form more complicated structures in discoverable ways. Though atomic theory, when considered in this way, has developed through too long a period to make it reasonable to talk about revolution, Katz's comparison does raise questions about the long-term status of the underlying realities that Chomsky talks about. Electron microscopes now allow us to observe some of the underlying realities that were originally philosophic conjectures: is there a similar possibility with respect to Chomsky's claims about the underlying realities of language?

This question suggests another comparison. Is Chomsky's theory anything like Freud's theory of the unconscious mind? Chomsky believes that his work has begun to show us something about psychological structures and processes that underlie language, and he admits that much of this structure and process is unconscious and, in the main, probably cannot be brought into conscious thought. Similarly, over half a century ago Freud postulated an unconscious mind, with unconscious drives, emotions, thoughts and structures, such as the *id* and *superego,* and he believed that much of this unconscious experience was in principle beyond what could be part of our ordinary conscious thoughts or feelings. However, after more than fifty years of Freudian psychology, most psychologists are quite skeptical about the reality of the underlying, unconscious structures that Freud wrote about. There does not seem to be any way of determining whether these unconscious structures are just the invention of Freudian psychologists or whether they have some further "underlying reality." The Freudian movement split into various factions, each postulating different sorts of unconscious structures, and gradually most scientists came to suspect that these hypothetical structures were not going to provide the precise and ever-deepening explanations of surface behavior that, in an analogous way, the notion of atomic elements provided for chemistry.

I agree that there is some justice in comparing the direction of recent work in linguistics with the move toward atomic theory in chemistry, and there is some justice in the worries expressed by comparing Chomsky with Freud. But I think the differences are interesting and important too. I do not think that we will ever be able to observe experimentally the underlying reality that linguistic theory now talks about in the way that we have become able to observe molecular and atomic particles. On the other hand, Chomsky's speculations about the psychological realities underlying language seem much more open to genuine, though indirect, test, correction, and discovery than theories like Freud's. As we work through a more specific comparison with Einstein's revolution, particularly keeping in mind the seven points I have listed, the question of evaluation will arise again and again: are we on our way to a deeper and more systematic understanding of how the human mind works or are we fooling ourselves?

CHAPTER 1

Traditional and Modern Language Study

WHAT is a language? Or, to put a related and more focused question, What is linguistics? that is, what belongs to the systematic, scientific study of language? Or, to bring both questions together, What is an *adequate linguistic description* of a language?

These are the difficult questions that modern scientific linguists have asked in order to distinguish their work from the traditional study of language and from the work of other sciences that are concerned with language in some way—for example, philosophy, psychology, mathematics and logic, sociology, anthropology, computer engineering, and so on (the list could be made quite long because language is involved crucially in nearly every human activity). These questions were given quite a narrow answer by recent linguists—particularly the structuralists —and the attempt to state this narrow view in a precise way led Chomsky to his discoveries.

I *Traditional Language Study: Literary, Historical, Prescriptive*

The study of language is as old and as diverse as history. Indeed, until the general spread of literacy over the past hundred years, the mark of the educated man was simply that he knew how to read and write some language, and the primary object of his studies was to do both well.

The traditional study of language was mostly concerned with the *written* language—with the letters, words, sentences, passages, of writing and printing, and with the proper ways of combining these items. Partly this was a result of technical difficulties hindering the study of spoken language. But more it was a lack of studious interest in what everyone could do without much trouble or any formal education. Why *study* what everyone knew without instruction, that is, how to speak his native language? Of course, it is this intense interest in "what everyone can do" that characterizes modern linguistics, whether structuralist or Chomskyan.

Modern linguists take the *spoken* language as their primary concern and they regard the written language as (mostly) derivative. Written language, that is, is essentially a mere writing-down of the spoken language. This seems a natural position to take, surely. Many human languages have no written forms and all human languages were spoken long before methods of transcribing were developed. And the items and combination rules of the written language are essentially the same as those of the spoken language.

One can only say "*essentially* the same" of course. Written letters do not correspond exactly with the spoken (phonemic) alphabet. The sentences, or strings of words (morphemes) bounded by silence, that we find normal in spoken English are somewhat different from normal written English (even leaving aside the extraneous noise, the "ahs" and "ums," of speech that disappear when we put pen or typewriter to use). But modern linguists do not find these differences very important. This is particularly true because modern linguists are concerned not with *excellence* in speech or writing but with the basic norm, and because modern linguists are almost exclusively concerned with no linguistic structure *larger than the sentence* (*words* and *sentences* can be spoken or written indifferently but this is not true of conversations, speeches, paragraphs, monographs, and so on).

Again, because of a practical lack of interest in "what everyone can do," traditional language study tended to be historical (or *diachronic*). When not concerned with excellence in writing or speech, traditional language study was concerned with authenticating written documents and interpreting ancient texts, with tracing origins and changes in word use, and charting the branching, lending, and changing that occurred as the modern languages of Europe developed from classical sources. Though they consider such studies linguistic and have done much to make such diachronic studies more extensive, systematic, and accurate, modern linguists emphasize that the first, or primary, level of description is nonhistorical (*synchronic*). The language must first be described as it exists at *one time* (synchronic = "same-time"), that is, as a system that ordinary speakers can know without having any idea of its previous history, of the original meanings of particular words, and so on.

Traditional students of language sometimes talked as if words "really mean" what they meant at some favored period in history, even going so far as to insist that many English words, for example, now "really mean" what the Greek and Latin words, from which they derived, meant in Greek texts from a few centuries before Christ's birth and in Latin texts from the two centuries surrounding Christ's birth. It is hard to take this idea seriously. Why should not the words in the Greek or Latin classical texts "really mean" not what they apparently meant there but what they meant in still earlier texts from which they derived? For that matter, why look to classical Latin rather than medieval (church) Latin? The only plausible answer goes back to a certain bias against "what everyone can do." The educated man was familiar with the classical texts, and for him they represented a standard of excellence and correctness. He wished to know his language not as "everyone" but as a literate man, who knew, for example, that *sentence* derived from a verb that meant to sense or know in Cicero's Latin—if it meant something else for graffiti writers or low-level bureaucrats of the same period, that was something beyond what a literate man should know.

The classical and literary bias of traditional language study was not only a matter of words. From medieval until recent times, the educated European was taught to describe the grammar of languages in terms derived from the study, and teaching, of Latin. Even today, for example, we talk of *past*, *present*, and *future tenses* (or *verb* forms) as if, as *is* true in Latin, English verbs had three forms. But English does not have *future* tense verb forms in the way that it does have *past* tense forms ("I see you tomorrow" is not a future *form* of the verb any more than "I see you"—it is the adverb tomorrow that makes the difference, for the verb does not change in form).

Talk about the historical and literary bias (particularly toward classical Greek and Latin) leads us to a third aspect of traditional language study: it is *prescriptive.* In a great many different ways, traditional language study was concerned with trying to work out how one *ought* to write or speak, in teaching ways of using language that are *excellent* (proper, polite, logical, poetic, graceful, convincing, upper-class) rather than just *describing* how people actually speak when speaking their language in a normal way. For example, modern linguists would consider prescriptive the claim of some traditionalists that the words *irregardless* and *ain't* do not belong to the English language. It is true that "irregardless" is an illogical word, because people who use the word mean "regardless" (both prefix and suffix— *ir-* and *-less*—reverse the meaning, and using both is redundant). It is also true that *ain't* is not found in formal speech and writing, and one runs the risk of being considered illiterate or "lower-class" if one uses it in ordinary conversation. (Note that there is not anything illogical about *ain't*; in origin it is a variant contraction of *am not.*) The modern linguist agrees that there are various dialects of English and that word and construction choice do differ according to context, social class, occupation, and so on; but he is not primarily concerned with such variations and he does not see it as his job to say which variations are desirable or undesirable.

Of course, one does have to be careful here. The distinction between *prescription* and *description* is not always a very clear or very useful one (as we shall see later, Chomsky himself has been accused of a prescriptive approach to language). What must be said, I think, is that anyone who talks on a general level about how language is used is talking about what kind of language use is *standard* or *regular* in *some group.* But regular and some group introduce problems that can always lead to the claim that a prescriptive element has entered into the discussion. Let us briefly consider both factors.

Regular suggests *according-to-rule,* and its opposite is not *unusual* but *not-according to rule.* No linguist can hope (or wants) to describe literally everything that comes out of the mouths of members of some group or even out of one person's mouth. In the first place, a great deal that comes out will not have anything to do with the group's language. People whistle, hum, burp, giggle, snort, snore, and so on without doing anything linguistic (such sounds could be a regular part of some language, of course); people sometimes speak languages foreign to their group or imitate speakers of other dialects. The linguist has to ignore these matters as outside the regular body of verbal practices that make up the language of the group. In the second place, when people do speak their language, a great deal of what comes out of their mouths is *irregular* or *nonregular*.

When people talk they often make unintended slips, hesitations, repetitions; they will agree if asked what they have said contains a slip or irregularity. Linguists often observe that such slips are usually unnoticed by both speaker and hearer because they are outside the normal regularities of the language. There is all the difference in the world between irregular and unusual sentences. Sentences (1), (2), and (3) below are *usual*, in the sense that people have made such slips on several occasions, but they are irregular; (4), (5), and (6) are unusual, in the sense that probably no one has ever said them (until now) in the entire history of English, but they are perfectly regular. (Linguists star irregular sentences.)

    *(1) The the salt is on the table
    *(2) Did you get the ahm......?
    *(3) These fish is the best
    (4) The last moon rock I bought cost less than sixty-five cents
    (5) Ferdinand Fagboot married Brigitte Bardot on the North Pole early in 1973
    (6) This is the blue-point Siamese that scratched the Professor of Sanscrit who is tutoring that albino boy whom you met in Budapest last August during that nit-picking conference on flea diseases

It is a notable fact about natural languages, such as English, that most of the (regular) sentences of a given language will never in fact be uttered. Aside from short, useful sentences such as "Pass the salt" and "Move over," a large portion of the sentences that a person utters on any given day have never been uttered (or written) before in the history of the English language. (Chomsky has emphasized these points about natural languages, and the reader who doubts their truth will be satisfied by formal arguments in a few pages.)

Not only does the linguist ignore *irregularities* but he also must discount *nonregularities*. As the use of "voice-prints" in the law courts suggests, every member of a linguistic group speaks his language slightly differently; and even the same person will say the same sentence slightly differently every time he repeats it (if delicate enough instruments are used to detect this). When I say that (6) is *a* sentence of English, I am talking about a *type*: the *class* that consists of all the different ways this *one* sentence could be written, typed, printed, and so on. In the same way, I can say that 246,000 is *one* particular number in the system of natural numbers, however it is written, typed, spoken, and so on. Most of what comes out of our mouths is nonregular in that it could be different without changing the sentence that we utter, without changing what is regular, or according to rule, in what we say.

I said that anyone who talks on a general level about how language is used is talking about what kind of language use is regular in some group. One can see how the notion of regularity can lead to the accusation that the linguist is being prescriptive, rather than purely descriptive. The linguist ignores nonregularities, labels certain forms irregular, and talks not only about what is regular in what people actually say but also about what *would be* regular if they got around to saying it. The linguist, to introduce a term of Chomsky's, is first concerned with linguistic *competence*, not with the nonregularities and irregularities of actual performance; the linguist is concerned with an ideal type, the completely competent speaker-hearer. If the label "prescriptive" is intended as a criticism, it can only be because the linguist's concept of competence does not jive with the practice and judgments of ordinary speakers. The *grammar*, in which the linguist lays out his notion of what constitutes competence in a particular language, predicts that the speakers of the language will find various sentences regular and others irregular; if the linguist's grammar fails in its predictions, it is defective (either simply because the linguist is mistaken or because he wants to improve the group's way of speaking). Any grammar is prescriptive in the sense that it projects (beyond the actual data) judgments of what is regular, nonregular, and irregular; an adequate grammar is one that faithfully predicts the intuitions of the ordinary language user about these matters. An adequate grammar should generate all and only those sentences which ordinary speakers find grammatically regular.

But there is still another problem about prescription versus description. I said that anyone who talks on a general level about how language is used is talking about what kind of language use is regular in some group. But what are the limits on "some group"?

What I have in mind is this. Suppose a traditional student of language tells us that *irregardless* and *ain't* are irregular or do not belong to the English language. We reply that "irregardless" is in common use among the group of people who speak (and write) English and that most English speakers will not mark a sentence with that word ungrammatical or irregular, though we agree that the word is illogical. The traditionalist could then counter by saying: I'm not prescribing, *I'm simply saying how English is used by the group of* logical *English speakers.* Again, if we tell the traditionalist that *ain't* is in common use among English speakers, though we agree that it is irregular for many English speakers, particularly those who are highly educated (the "elite"), the traditionalist may counter by saying: *I'm not prescribing, I'm describing how English is used by the group of* elite *English speakers.*

If he is allowed to specify "some group" in any way he wants, particularly if we allow him to bring in speech contexts and linguistic structures larger than sentences, the traditionalist can introduce all the subjects and problems of traditional language study (plus many other matters). For example, traditional language study often became *literary criticism*, a study of versification and metaphor; or *rhetoric*, a study of persuasive use of language; or *logic*, a study of valid argument, of implication, contradiction, and logical truth. If asked to justify this, the traditional linguist could say that he was just describing what was regular language use in such groups as the highly literate, experienced public speakers, or among logicians and logical speakers.

If the traditionalist is allowed to talk not only about sentences and groups of sentences (poems, arguments, and so on) but also about *regularities between sentences and contexts* (loosely, about *meaning* or *semantics*), the traditionalist could talk about nearly anything. Knowledge of any fact about the world could become part of "linguistic competence" and part of the linguist's subject matter—because people's judgments of regularity (or decisions about ambiguity) can always be influenced by their factual knowledge. For example, sentences (7), (8), and (9) below seem to represent a progression in more and more complete impossibility. Given what we know about the world, all are irregular, or even meaningless, in the sense that no possible situation could correspond to them:

(7) A rattlesnake climbed straight up my leg
(8) Here is a round, triangular cube that is red and green all over
(9) Colorless green ideas sleep furiously

Sentence (7) is impossible because rattlesnakes cannot climb (at least in the sense of climbing straight up something); sentence (8) because cubes cannot be triangular, let alone round, and so on. But if we make the knowledge of rattlesnakes part of linguistic competence, nearly any sort of knowledge might be brought in. It might even be suggested that sentence (10) below should be marked regular or irregular depending on whether or not one is a member of the New Left; or that sentence (11) should be marked irregular unless the speaker has actually indicated where a chair is:

(10) John called Mary a Republican and then she insulted him
(11) Bring me that chair over there

As a corollary of the tendency of traditional language study to get mixed up with all sorts of different studies, a final characteristic of traditional language study should be mentioned, namely, traditional linguistics lacked precision and formalization. The traditionalist might, for example, define a sentence as "what expresses a complete thought," or a noun as "what names a person, place, or thing." But both definitions are imprecise.

There is certainly no step-by-step formal procedure for deciding whether something "expresses a complete thought"; "sincerity" is a noun and "sincere" is an adjective—does it really make sense to say that the first form "names a person, place or thing" while the second does not do so? Generally, traditionalists gave descriptions of languages that depended heavily on the good sense and intuitions of the reader: such descriptions were unclear and incomplete.

II *Structural Linguistics: Practice and Problems*

Modern linguistics—indeed the very words *linguistics* and *scientific linguistics*—arose from a desire to distinguish linguistics (and hence its subject matter, language) and the adequate description of language, from other sciences and subject matters. In doing so, the modern linguist does not mean to say that traditional language study was mostly nonsense or mistaken, but rather that it was imprecise and unclear, confused with all sorts of other studies. The modern linguist wanted to be able to study his subject without having to make assumptions about other subjects (psychology, logic, and so on). It was not that the modern linguist thought that these other subjects were plagued with superstition, but because he wanted his results to be available to other sciences without prejudice, that is, without including along with the linguistic data, perhaps covertly, assumptions about these other sciences. He did not regard it as his job to tell the psychologist and logician, or literary critic and status seeker, what to believe about their own subject matters.

Specifically, the modern linguist is primarily concerned with linguistic regularities concerning sentences and their constituents, particularly in spoken language, currently in use in some group that is not marked off in any way involving economic status, education, or not-narrowly-linguistic abilities. He is concerned, in other words, with "what everyone can do" who speaks English, German, Swahili, or any other human language.

Still more narrowly, many modern linguists have wanted to say that a *language* (as types of regularities found in a group) could be defined as follows:

(A) A language is a set of sentences.

A *sentence* could then be defined as (B) (using the linguist's rough technical equivalent for word, morpheme):

(B) A sentence is a string of morphemes.

We could expand (B) to indicate that the morphemes, or words, are from the *lexicon* (dictionary) of the language in question, and the string, of course, is one that belongs to the set of sentences composing the language. Finally, since the hundreds of thousands of words found in any natural language break down into *phonemes* (the rough spoken equivalents of written letters), there is another level of sentence structure, (C).

(C) A sentence is a string of phonemes.

In that all natural language sentences have the "duality of structure" indicated by (B) and (C), modern linguists have distinguished *two* jobs in the identification and classification of linguistic items that compose sentences: *phonemics* and *morphemics*. The linguist's job, when setting out to describe a language, is to identify the phonemes, and latterly the morphemes, of a language, indicating possible combinations of these items. The assumption was that these items had a purely physical reality as noise that could be adequately described without bringing in the human beings who used the language.

Indeed, from a methodological point of view, many modern linguists have thought that a linguist, with a few hundred hours of tapes of a language previously unknown to the linguist, ought to be able to identify first the phonemes and then the morphemes of the sentences of the taped *corpus* (body of data). This view is particularly characteristic of those linguists who wanted to get as far from traditional language study as possible: the *structuralists*. I shall end this section by giving a brief account of the structuralists, for they exemplify modern linguists in the most extreme sense, and Chomsky's work begins within many of their assumptions, such as (A), (B), and (C), even though his work sharply criticizes some of their claims.

Structuralist linguistics received its basic exposition in Leonard Bloomfield's *Language* (1933); its most recent distinguished expression is found in Zellig Harris's *Methods in Structural Linguistics* (1951). Bloomfield makes very clear a general commitment, both for psychology and linguistics, to behaviorism, to the view that scientific descriptions of human beings should be confined to their perceived behavior, to what a scientist could observe and measure directly. In both Bloomfield and Harris one finds an implicit commitment to behaviorism in that they believe that the primary job of characterizing a language, through phonemic and morphemic analysis, can be adequately achieved in principle through working with a corpus, a body of noise that can be broken down into linguistic "atoms" and "molecules" without bringing in questions about meaning or human psychology.

Harris ended his *Methods in Structural Linguistics* by suggesting that the linguistic data about a particular language, discovered through following his suggested methods, could be formulated in a "grammar of lists." Though this is somewhat simpler than what Harris specifically had in mind, I think it fair enough to say that his suggested grammar would consist of the following lists:

I. A list of phonemes and of restrictions on where they occur in sequences (examples: ordinary English does not contain the "ch" sound in the Scottish word "loch"; the two phonemes that begin words such as *squalid, squat,* and *squaw* must always be followed by a liquid sound here represented by "u").

II. A list of morphemes and restrictions on where they occur in sequences (examples: *with* occurs in the context *played——her* but *of* does not).

III. A list of phrases and restrictions on their combination, ultimately specifying the possible sentences. (Note that we ideally have here a series of levels of analysis, each concerning successively longer units that can be defined in terms of the level below—one particular morpheme is just one particular sequence of phonemes and vice versa.)

It would be the job of *phonology* to produce list (I); *syntax* and *morphology* would take care of (II) and (III).

As an example one might think about the letter and word construction games that are now available (*Scrabble*®, for instance). Imagine that we observe some people who speak a language unknown to us playing a game like *Scrabble*®. Our first job as structural linguists would be to figure out how many distinguishable symbols they have (it is much easier to imagine doing this with a visual, rather than an auditory, alphabet). Then we try to figure out which symbols can be placed together in sequence and which cannot. If we succeed in doing this, we would seem to have the equivalent, in our example, of the phonology of the language. (If we wanted to make our task more difficult, and more like that of a genuine linguist, we could imagine that the letters could be written in various ways, so that one could not be at all sure, at first, whether two letters were the same, that is, both instances of the same type of letter.)

Next imagine that our natives play a word game in which words are combined rather than letters. Our first task would be to identify the different words, the vocabulary or lexicon, of the game. This would be difficult if the graphic conventions followed in writing the words were quite loose (imagine, for example, that the cubes had words on them written by people with quite different handwriting). Of course, if the natives are still playing with the same language, our problem would be solved in that *we have already identified the alphabet* of the language. For example, we could tell that *hand* and *HAND* were instances of the same word, or morpheme, because we established in the previous game that *h* is the same letter, or phoneme, as *H*, *a* the same as *A*, and so on.

If after observing the game for a time (in a manner analogous to the structural linguist working with a *corpus*) we were able to identify the alphabet and vocabulary of the moves by the players, we would then be able to take any of the moves (sentences) made and give it *an adequate linguistic description*. We would have, in other words, a list of the phonemes, and an associated list for each such "letter" of all the variations in graphic appearance; we would also have a list of morphemes, each written in our phonemic alphabet, so that variations in graphic appearance would be recognized by consulting our phonemic list. Given, then, a particular sentence (or move) we would be able to identify it as a string of phonemes (as in [C]) and as a string of morphemes (as in [B]). Further, we might identify common sequences of morphemes, or phrases—traditionally called parsing a sentence.

Notice that what we are able to do with a sentence is to identify and classify its elements at various levels. This approach to linguistics has been called *taxonomical*; similarly, the job of classifying animals into species, species into genera, genera into families, and so on, is called taxonomy. Given a sentence (move), we simply identify or classify its elements at various levels, as, for example, in Figure I, where three different ways of giving the same description are indicated (with bracketing, an "up side down" tree diagram, or an indication of combination at each level using "+").

[[my] [father]] [[loves]] [[old] [men] [and] [women]]

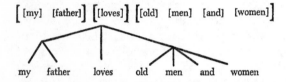

my   father   loves   old   men   and   women

my father + loves + old men and women   (phrase level)
my + father + loves + old + men + and + women   (word level)
m+y+f+a+t+h+e+r+l+o+v+e+s+o+l+d+m+e+n+a+n+d+w+o+m+e+n

(phonemic level)

FIGURE 1

We now have before us a very rough picture of how the structuralist linguist ideally proposes to go about his business of taxonomically describing the sentences of a corpus. But—and this is one of the main points of giving these game examples—there are many questions one might ask about this procedure, whether the questions are raised about the game examples or about the analogous procedure of giving a genuine phonemic, morphemic, etc., analysis of a taped corpus.

There is a *procedural question*: why not simply ask the game players (or the speakers of a taped corpus) what the alphabet and vocabulary are, and what instances of letters and words are the same or different?

There is a *projective question*: what relationship is there between the corpus and the language, assuming that ultimately we are interested in the whole language rather than in the corpus itself?

There is the *question of formulation*. After listing the alphabet and vocabulary of the games (or corpus), we are supposed to indicate what items occur with some, but not with other, items: but how is that occurrence supposed to be indicated?

Finally, there is a *question of adequacy*: how do we tell whether our description is really adequate? Specifically, how do we know that we have got the right number of levels? And how, more specifically, can we assign levels and bracketing higher than the word level?

II.I *Procedure: how to ask the natives*

The questions of projection, formulation, and adequacy are the questions that Chomsky asked of structural linguistics. Once these questions about language in general were asked, the approach taken by the structuralists to the study of particular languages, specifically, of the corpora drawn from these languages, came to seem clearly inadequate, even on structuralist terms. The "methods" of the structural linguists were supposed to be appropriate for the study of any language that humans might speak, without including in any way assumptions about human psychology, or foisting on the linguist dubious views about "universal" features of language. The structuralists were particularly sensitive to the tendency of traditional linguists to describe new languages in terms and categories derived from European languages (or more narrowly, from Latin), and they wanted to describe each language as a unique system without any presumptions about other languages. Indeed, the choice of the label "structuralist" is sometimes explained by saying that the elements that concern the linguist—phonemes, morphemes, phrases—have no reality outside the regularities of their positions within *structures* (i.e., sentences). In principle, any similarity between the phonemes, morphemes, and phrases of one language and others is just accidental. For example, in Chinese our "r" and "l" sounds are not distinct phonemes, but are one sound in terms of Chinese sentence structures; and hence Chinese speakers of English may not hear the difference between *fried rice* and *flied lice*. Equally, we do not make phonemic distinctions in pitch that the speaker of Chinese makes. Though many languages have many phonemes in common, each language has its own unique phonemic alphabet which should be derived just from describing the language (or corpus) by itself.

What Chomsky came to show by asking his questions was that structuralist "methods" actually were, in effect, *theories* about the general nature of human language and about how language could be described adequately. Once the questions were pressed far enough, it became clear that the methods in question could not achieve adequate descriptions and that the tacit theory about human language was false. It is perhaps a measure of Chomsky's success that present editions of Harris's book are titled just *Structural Linguistics,* the word "Methods" having been dropped; and that linguists now write books and teach courses about *language* without the *−s,* about "theoretical linguistics," "the abstract theory of language," "universal grammar," and "universal phonetic theory."

The questions of projection, formulation, and adequacy led to the suggestion that procedure be changed; and, more abstractly, that the presuppositions—behaviorism and empiricism—that underlay structuralist procedure be changed. So let us begin by asking again the first of our questions. Why not simply ask the game players (or speakers of a corpus) what the alphabet and vocabulary are, and what instances of letters and words (or phonemes and morphemes) are the same or different?

The general answer of the structuralist is that he is concerned with what people are doing and *not* with what people *think* they are doing. This general answer, of course, emphasizes the structuralist's commitment to empiricism and, more specifically, to behaviorism, that is, he is committed to the view that science should be concerned only with what is observable, and thus that the human sciences should deal with observed human behavior rather than with "subjective" thoughts and feelings. More specifically, the structuralist would say that people's judgments about what they are doing are in principle essentially irrelevant. The linguist is describing objective noise, a physical phenomenon which *does*, in the cases that interest the linguist, *happen to exhibit certain regularities*, that is, certain species, genera, and families of noises that regularly appear in certain patterns. Admittedly, speaker-hearers of the language are aware of some of these regularities and may be able to give the linguist revealing hints about them, but the structuralist insists that since what he is describing has objective existence quite apart from what people may think, quite apart from psychology, he ought to be able to describe it without asking what people think. There is another, less theoretical, reason why the structuralist wants to discover the grammar of a language without asking the native speakers questions, namely, they will very likely give misleading or false answers.

The native speaker is not a linguist and so cannot be expected to understand or answer accurately questions about what are the minimal sound units (phonemes) and minimal grammatical units (morphemes) of his language. Many studies have shown that ordinary language users are likely to "hear" distinctions in sound that are not there in fact or to mistake variant pronunciations of a phoneme for more significant differences. If we do teach the native speaker structural linguistics, he will then become more accurate but he will be in no better position than the nonnative linguist. Indeed, he may be in a worse position because his cultural attitudes—about status, etiquette, meaning, and so on—may bias his descriptions. After all, we would be hesitant about accepting conclusions reached by a psychologist examining his own psychology, by a doctor diagnosing his own illness, and so on.

Of course, there are limits to this skepticism. Aside from accepting the corpus itself as a largely regular set of sentences, the linguist may use his ingenuity in "eliciting" new sentences. The corpus may lead the linguist to wonder whether or not a certain sentence is regular, or grammatical. The difficulty then is to see if one can put the native speaker in such a position that he will say the sentence (or indicate that it is regular) only if it is regular. The real problem of "elicitation" is that of ensuring that one does not prejudice the issue: there is a risk that the native speaker will say something irregular to please the linguist, or from confusion, and so on; equally there is a

risk that he will reject a sentence not because it is ungrammatical
but because it is (in the physical context) false, silly, impolite,
obscene, impossible, and so on.

A structuralist who wants to be very strict would suggest
that elicited sentences are simply part of the corpus. The structuralist wants to preserve the independence of linguistic descriptions from the judgments of language users about what they
think they are saying or hearing. In theory, when the linguist
elicits a sentence, he is not asking the native speaker whether
the sentence is, or is not, grammatical; the structural linguist
is not asking the informant for any sort of judgment about
language. Rather he is placing the native speaker in a position
where he will naturally tend to say the sentence if it is grammatical and refuse to say the sentence if it is not grammatical.
However, a structuralist probably would accept generalization
(D)—at least if he is allowed to drop the parenthetical addition
and, perhaps, to rewrite "tendency to accept" in more explicitly behavioral terms.

(D) An adequate linguistic description of a language should
account for the native speaker's tendency to accept, or
not accept, certain sentences as part of his language
(i.e., to account for his judgments that sentences are,
or are not, grammatical).

But though one can understand the structuralist reason, in
principle and practice, for mistrusting native speakers' linguistic
judgments, one may well wonder why structuralists have been
so urgently concerned with elicitation, so worried about biasing
the native speaker's responses, so taken up in general with what
have been called *discovery procedures*.

There is one special reason for the strength of this concern.
Structuralism has been above all adopted by American linguists,
and these linguists have usually spent some portion of their
graduate study, if not a good portion of their professional life,
in the study of American Indian languages. In the first half
of this century, many of these languages remained undescribed
or inadequately described, very few had any written form or
transcribed record, and the speakers of many of these languages
were old and few. If there is, in the extreme case, only one

speaker of a language, it is no wonder that the linguist will want to be extremely careful about elicitation, about biasing the speaker's response, about careful discovery procedures.

Obviously, if I am working on a language with hundreds of thousands of speakers, whose culture and way of life is not too different from my own, I will not worry so much about biasing my native informant, nor about misunderstanding his reactions (particularly, whether he rejects a sentence because it is not grammatical or for some extraneous cultural reason). But if I am working with the last speaker of some American Indian language, I will want to be much more careful. If I bias his responses, I may very well have changed his language unwittingly. If, through some procedural error on my part, I elicit a sentence that did not belong to his language, there is no way to check the data because there are no other speakers, and my informant may now act as if the sentence is part of his language because of his experience with me. Again, since I may have difficulties understanding his culture and way of life, I am much more likely to be confused as to whether he accepts or rejects elicitation because the sentence is (or is not) part of his language, or for extraneous reasons of culture, belief, or social context.

The problem of single (or few) informants may suggest another reason why structuralists saw their problem more as that of giving an adequate description of a (possibly taped) corpus, rather than of the whole language. If a language has but one speaker and no written texts, what he says is all there is to that language (at least in explicit observational terms): his speech, the corpus that he produces, is the language.

Incidentally, the structuralist's concern with not biasing the informant's response, with pure description of the informant's behavior that excludes his judgments about it, led some structuralists to feel that European languages posed for linguists the sorts of difficulties that domesticated animals pose for biological taxonomists. The linguistic behavior, especially under elicitation, of the speaker of, say, English would not be "pure" because the ordinary speaker of English, particularly one who is generally well educated, will have been taught traditional "prescriptive" grammar while at school. His way of speaking will be partly a natural product and partly irregularly distorted by half-remembered "rules of proper speech," as domestic animals, too, are distorted from natural development by human attempts to "improve" them. Imperious popular book titles such as *Leave Your Language Alone!* are a product of some linguist's irritation with European languages whose colloquial bases are overlaid with various attempts, pressed by school teachers and traditional grammarians, to "correct" and "improve" speech. But though the structuralist may become annoyed (if he studies such languages at all) with informants whose responses are influenced by their sense of what constitutes competent speech against the "mistakes" or "informality" of their everyday speech performance, he must admit that the distinction between competence, or ideal speech, and actual performance is surely a fairly universal feature of human language.

Here this special concern with accurately preserving the many dying Indian languages comes together with the structuralist's general tendency toward behaviorism and empiricism. For the study of American Indian languages was part of a general interest in cultural anthropology by structural linguists; an interest in anthropology that also insisted on studying a native's *behavior* and not engaging in unscientific speculations about his thought.

The father of scientific cultural anthropology, Bronislaw Malinowski, demanded that the anthropologist above all study the literal physical behavior of natives, understanding this behavior as a network of customs that gradually came about through the natural selection of practices that helped fulfill basic biological needs (without requiring the postulation of any conscious thought on the part of particular natives). Here the natural desire of any anthropologist (or field linguist) to avoid mistakenly imposing on the natives his own Western categories and ways of thought and to concentrate instead on the "objective" biological activity of the natives jells with the behaviorist conviction that talking about how people think is really just a fuzzy way of talking about the patterns found in their behavior. Since this meant that the native's thought, his way of looking at the world, was going to be just as arbitrary and unique as his behavior and as the phonemes and morphemes of his language, it was best for the investigator to confine science to a careful study of observed behavior. The basic conviction, shared by structuralist and Malinowskian scholars, who dominated linguistics and anthropology in the 1930's and 1940's, was that each culture and language was a unique and arbitrary system of activity and way of slicing up the world. Hence the term *cultural relativism,* which labels the view that such systems cannot be rated one above another, in part or as a whole, because all such ratings are relative to particular cultural assumptions and there are no significant cultural (or linguistic) universals (that is, assumptions universally found in human cultures).

And so one sees that the structuralist's special interest in accurately preserving American Indian languages, and with helping anthropologists generally with similar acts of preservation, reinforced the structuralist's general behaviorist prejudice when studying behavior against considering what people think they are doing. The connection between special interest and general conviction is particularly seen in the structuralist tendency to assume that his primary job is the description of a corpus, of what some people have actually said, rather than of a language in the broadest sense of what people might say. In the case of the last hours of the last speaker of a language, it does make reasonable sense to equate the corpus with the language: these last taped sentences are all there ever will be of the language. But this does not seem a reasonable view in general. Generally, we take it for granted that a corpus—some recorded sentences whether taped by a genuine linguist or from our imagined letter and word games—is just a tiny sample of all the sentences that speakers of a language have produced, which in turn is just a sample of all the sentences that they will or might produce. We return to the projective question: what relationship is there between the corpus and the language?

II. II *Projection: corpus and language*

If, for example, we had tapes of spoken English—perhaps several hundred hours of telephone conversations—there would obviously be a large number of perfectly grammatical sentences missing from our corpus. It is quite unlikely that we would find sentences (4), (5), and (6) in our corpus!

(4) The last moon rock I bought cost less than sixty-five cents

(5) Ferdinand Fagboot married Brigette Bardot on the North Pole early in 1973

(6) This is the blue-point Siamese that scratched the Professor of Sanscrit who is tutoring that albino boy whom you met in Budapest last August during that nit-picking conference on flea diseases

And I think, as I said a few pages back, that it is likely that even if we recorded every bit of spoken (or written) English prior to my invention of these instances, we still would not find these sentences. Even if these sentences, by some extraordinary chance, should happen to have been actually spoken at some time, it is easy enough to see that there must be large numbers of hitherto unspoken (or unwritten) sentences that English speakers would agree would be perfectly good English sentences if they were actually spoken or written.

During human history English speakers have produced a very large but *finite* number of English sentences. How many sentences of English remain unspoken (such as [4], [5], and [6])? Chomsky has a surprising and perfectly definite answer: *an infinite number of sentences*. This answer derived from what I call *Chomsky's axiom*:

(E) A natural language consists of an infinite number of sentences.

That an infinite number of English sentences remain unspoken follows from this axiom because subtracting a finite number, such as the number of sentences that have already been spoken, from an infinite number always leaves an infinite number.

Let me try to explain why Chomsky holds that a natural language such as English is a set consisting of an infinite number of sentences. The vocabulary of English is finite. It has to be learned item by item so that a speaker could only know it if it were finite (similarly for the much smaller phonemic alphabet). And if our knowledge of English involves knowing (or at least unconsciously following) rules or principles for constructing sentences, there must be a finite number of them, too, if we are to have learned them. If a natural language does consist of an infinite number of sentences, how can we, who have finite vocabularies and rules to work with, know such natural languages? The answer is that many of the rules, or principles, that may be followed in constructing English sentences, whether by a native speaker or by a linguist projecting accurately from a corpus, are *recursive*. Recursive rules are those that can be applied over and over and over and over again indefinitely (for example, the rule that one can add "and over" in between "over" and "again" is repeated again and again and again in the preceding sentence, and there does not seem to be any rule limiting repetition of the rule to any particular number).

Consider (12), (13), and (14) as examples of recursion at work. In each case, the rules that create the sentences could be repeated again and again.

(12) This is the man who owned the dog that chased the cat that ate the rat that nipped the mouse that stole the cheese that came from the man who ...

(13) "There's cold chicken inside it," replied the Rat briefly, "cold tongue, cold ham, cold beef, pickled gherkins, salad, French rolls, cress sandwiches, potted meat, ginger beer, lemonade, soda water—" (Kenneth Grahame, *The Wind in the Willows*)

(14) The courthouse is less old than the town, which began somewhere under the turn of the century as a Chickasaw Agency trading-post and so continued for almost thirty years before it discovered, not that it lacked a depository for its records and certainly not that it needed one, but that only by creating or anyway decreeing one, could it cope with a situation which otherwise was going to cost somebody money . . . (William Faulkner, *Requiem for a Nun*; with some dialogue interruptions, this sentence continues for the entire book.)

Although longer forms of these sentences are rare—because people can easily become bored or lose track—*one can see no reason to stop at any particular point*, any more than there is some natural stopping point if we ask someone to count out the natural numbers. The person we ask to count may stop the sequence at 23, or 63, or whatever, but we all know that he *could* go on forever—in the sense that there is an infinite number of numbers in the sequence, each just as much a number as the other and each generated by the rules of counting, though we know that any human being would have to stop from exhaustion at some point. Similarly, the Rat could go on and on, no matter how many items there are in the luncheon basket; and William Faulkner did go on for something like 25,000 words.

In general, our language allows us to embed one sentence within another, and then still another within the sentence we just generated, and yet another on to infinity, each time following the same construction principle (as in [12]); even more simply, our language allows us to join one sentence after another to form larger sentences merely by use of the conjunction *and*; and, of course, there are a very large number of cases in which one can go on adding nouns, adjectives, etc., indefinitely in series of such words (as in [13]). Of course, it is clear in general that the longer sentences get, the less likely it is that we will actually use them, but that is equally true of sequences of higher numbers. Just as it is unlikely that anyone ever said or wrote sentences (4), (5), and (6) before I did, so it is unlikely that anyone ever said or wrote 198,067,976,347,450,943, following it with that number plus one, and that in turn plus one, and so on. Yet we immediately recognize that (4), (5), and (6) are grammatical sentences (as opposed to the enormous number of nonsentences I could have produced by arbitrarily stringing the same words together) and we immediately recognize the number I just wrote as a natural number (i.e., a positive whole number) as opposed to the infinitely greater number of numerical expressions that I might have written.

Speaking strictly, too, the number of natural numbers that have not yet been actually produced by human beings (or machines) is infinite, just as is the number of unproduced grammatical English sentences. Any human being, or any computer, will produce only a finite number of numbers, whether by speaking, writing or printing out. But the number of human beings and computers is finite and adding together a finite number of finite numbers still produces only a finite number, and any such finite number of numbers, if removed from the infinity of natural numbers, will leave an infinity of numbers.

How do we know that there is an infinity of natural numbers? Obviously, no one could list or actually count out the numbers. But we know that there is an infinite number of natural numbers because *we know how to generate* (count out by rule) the sequence of natural numbers. We know how to go on *recursively*. Given any natural number, we know the rule for producing the next one, that is, we simply add one to the number we have, add one to the new number, and so on and so on. Any number generated by the rule is a natural number, and since the rule for generating the next highest number applies to any number (however high), we know that there is no highest natural number and that the sequence of natural numbers is infinite. The point is that we can extend the sequence as far as we wish by a simple recursive rule; similarly, we know that there is no highest prime number—that there are an infinite number of prime numbers—because a rule can be given for constructing a higher prime number, starting with any prime number we please.

Chomsky gives essentially the same answer to the question *How do we know that there are an infinite number of sentences in a natural language such as English?* Most of the sentences that we hear or utter each day are new to us, but we understand them because they are constructed by the same rules as the sentences we have already met up with.

But this knowledge leads to a different view about what language is and about what an adequate description of a language will involve. If a language consists of an infinite number of sentences, then the linguist cannot describe the language by listing its sentences. The only way in which an infinite set of sentences (or numbers) can be described is by giving the rules that generate the set in question. As Chomsky writes at the beginning of his first published book, *Syntactic Structures* (1957):

Syntax is the study of principles and processes by which sentences are constructed in particular languages. Syntatic investigation of a given language has as its goal the construction of a grammar that can be viewed as a device of some sort for producing the sentences of the language under analysis. (p. 11)

This definition may be contrasted with Zellig Harris's "summary of results" at the end of *Structural Linguistics*:

The preceding chapters have indicated a number of operations which can be carried out successively on the crude data of the flow of speech, yielding results which lead up to a compact statement of what utterances occur in the corpus. (p. 361)

Harris is, of course, aware that description of a corpus is not a description of a language. For Harris, description of a language is something quite beyond descriptive linguistics (except if the corpus included all the sentences that occur in a single speech community at a single time).

The structural linguist simply describes the corpus. If it is a "good" or "representative" sample, he assumes that phonemes, morphemes, and phrases (and sequences of such) that do not occur in the corpus probably will not occur in the language. Harris suggests explicitly that statistical probabilities come in here. From the description of the corpus, assuming we can establish on other grounds that our sample is good, we can derive the conclusion that certain possible sequences have some probability of occurrence, while others (what the nonstructuralist would call "ungrammatical") are quite improbable. This is what the structuralist takes to be the relationship between corpus and language. The language is the set of utterances that occur in a speech community at essentially one period of time; if the corpus drawn from this set by the linguist is a good sample, then statistical projections may be made about what will be found in the part of the set that was not included in the corpus. However, if Chomsky's axiom is correct, then there is something very dubious about this point of view. Let me try to show this.

Strictly speaking, if there is an infinite number of gram-matical English sentences and we assume (temporarily) that we are no more likely to produce one rather than another, then there is no significant probability assigned to *any* of these sentences. The point is that if there is an infinite number of possible sentences the probability that I will say some arbitrarily chosen sentence in some given time period is infinitely small. Consequently it seems hopeless to argue that what distinguishes sentences of the language from nonsentences is that it is more probable (this being projected from the corpus) that I will say any of the sentences rather than that I will say any of the nonsentences.

The probability that I should have produced sentence (6) is small beyond measure, no greater than that I should have produced a sentence of Chinese. Of course, since I do not know Chinese, I could not be said to have constructed a Chinese sentence as a speaker of Chinese would; I do not have a tacit knowledge of the "principles and processes by which sentences are constructed" in Chinese. But a structuralist is concerned with noise, not the (psychological or grammatical) processes of sentence construction. And the probability that I would have produced the *noise sequence* of (6) (before I did) seems just as close to zero as that I should have (quite unintentionally) produced the noise sequence that is, from a strict structuralist viewpoint, a particular Chinese sentence.

Moreover, so Chomsky has often argued, there is something wrong in general about regarding grammaticality as a variety of probability. Sentences (4), (5), and (6) are just as grammatical as (15) and (16), which is just to say that they are all grammatical. And this is true even though, had I not actually produced (4), (5), and (6), no one might ever have said them during the history of our language, while (15) and (16) are said by countless speakers of English every day:

(15) Pass the salt
(16) I'd like some water

Grammaticality just does not seem to be the sort of thing that one can measure quantitatively, like weight (leaving aside delicate and restricted stylistic questions about a relatively small number of forms). It seems as silly to say that (6), for example, is 99 percent grammatical (as opposed, perhaps, to the 100 percent grammaticality of (15)) as it does to say that 198,067,976,-

347,450,943 is 99 percent a natural number (as opposed, one supposes, to the 100 percent natural number character of, say, 211). Similarly, (17) is 100 percent ungrammatical, rather than being grammatical to some suitably small percentage point:

(17) Table chair sofa the very

The two natural numbers I wrote above are both natural numbers (as are any other natural numbers), because they were produced by the same "principles and processes," that is, because they were generated by the same recursive rule. The relationship between some corpus of spoken natural numbers (however large) and the infinite sequence of all the natural numbers is just this: they are both generated by the same recursion. By far the simplest and best way to describe a corpus (of, say, several hundred natural numbers) would be to give the ten digits (vocabulary) and then the rule for generating the sequence of natural numbers.

It would be far less simple and less than adequate to "describe" the corpus either by listing all the numbers in it individually or by summarizing this list in a way that made no distinction between what could or could not have occurred *and* what did or did not occur. While the second alternative might be shorter than the first, it would include purely *accidental* generalizations alongside the *essential* generalization that *only* numbers generated by the rule that generates the natural numbers will be found in the corpus. For example, the corpus might not *happen* to include any number between 499 and 591 or any number with 14 as its first digits; a strictly "structuralist" description of this corpus would need to state these purely accidental generalizations alongside the essential generalizations that follow from the rule generating the natural number sequence (for example, that 07, 0008, -7, 9.14, 3/4, and so on, are not found in the corpus).

Similarly, a structuralist linguist who attempts to describe a corpus through a "grammar of lists," fails to distinguish what happens not to occur (what is not part of the corpus) from what cannot occur (what is not part of the language), and this makes his job terribly difficult, if not impossible. As we have seen, it is absurd to regard the relationship between the corpus (given through a "grammar of lists") and the language as one of probability: it is absurd, that is, to say that the sentences of the language are all, and only, those sentences that have some minimal degree of probability of occurring on the basis of the actual occurrence of the corpus sentences. Rather, the corpus is adequately described insofar as its description has "as its goal the construction of a grammar that can be viewed as a device of some sort for producing the language under analysis." Just as with the natural numbers, the relationship between the corpus and the language is that both are generated by the same recursion. Just as in the mathematical case, it is in principle beside the point, and in any case needlessly difficult, to describe the *accidental* features of the corpus: one is interested in what can, or cannot, occur, not in what just happens to occur. Now, of course, what "can occur" is just what does occur in the infinite set of sentences that compose the language (and what "cannot occur" is what does not so occur), but since an infinite set cannot be listed, the only way it can be described is through giving "a device of some sort" that generates the language.

For Chomsky, the primary interest of the linguist is with specifying this "device of some sort" that *generates* the sentences of the language under analysis (or more generally any particular human language): this device will specify what is somehow "internalized" in the competent speaker-hearer of the language. Though the most usual label for Chomsky's general sort of linguistics is "transformational-generative linguistics," the most crucial word is "generative"—as opposed to "taxonomical"—since the primary concern is with the "principles and processes by which sentences are constructed in particular languages," not with the identification and classification of items found in the surface end product of these principles and processes.

In summary, though we may start with the assumption that a language is a set of sentences, since this set is infinite, it cannot be given as a list, that is, it cannot be enumerated. Consequently, even conceding the structuralist's contention that linguists should describe sentences and not speculate about the psychology of those who produce the sentences, we reach the conclusion nonetheless that a language cannot be described except by in effect specifying a "device of some sort" for generating the sentences of the language. Further, though we can list a corpus and give some sort of description of its sentences, we cannot derive the language from this corpus in terms of probabilities. If, indeed, we describe the corpus itself as generated by the right sort of generative device, this device will also generate the language, which means all the sentences that were only accidentally excluded from the corpus. Thus, still further and more specifically, one may argue that the corpus itself cannot be adequately described without bringing in the rest of the language, without bringing in the problem of specifying a "device of some sort."

I have so often quoted Chomsky's claim that linguistic description of a language has "as its goal the construction of a grammar that can be viewed as a device of some sort for producing the sentences of the language" that the reader may well ask, "Device of what sort?" I shall begin to answer this question by talking about the problem of *formulation,* which we raised some pages back, and about the problem of *adequacy,* which we have already met under the heading of *projection.* But the *whole* answer to this question is Chomsky's most basic concern, and therefore the subject matter of the rest of this book. Before going on with the formulation problem, it may help if we take a brief look ahead.

There are two aspects to the basic theme of the following chapters: (1) Human beings, speaking any given human language, are "devices of some sort" that generate the sentences of the given language; indeed, human beings are also "devices of some sort," or "language acquisition devices," for learning any human language they happen to be exposed to in their first few years of life. (2) The more we can show that the grammars of human languages must contain various features, the more we have shown that the human mind—as far as its linguistic capacities go—has these features. Again a mathematical example may be helpful. There are a great number of different ways to do arithmetic, to add, subtract, multiply, and divide, etc.; but mathematicians, working on the theory of abstract computing devices, have shown that a particularly simple and general sort of information sorting machine can do arithmetic as no simpler machine can; and so human beings, who can do arithmetic, are at least machines of this sort. Language, however, is a much more specific and detailed sort of phenomenon—one learned earlier and more thoroughly than arithmetic—hence the hope is that linguistics will give us a much more specific picture of what kind of a language-using device man is. The linguist is not a psychologist in a direct experimental sense, but the hope is that *he will be able to confine* his specification of the "device of some sort" that generates the language *so much* that he will tell us something about the human beings who also generate the language (though in ways that present experimental psychology or physiology cannot investigate directly).

Consider these two sets of boxes to represent, in parallel, what the linguist and ordinary person do when exposed to a language.

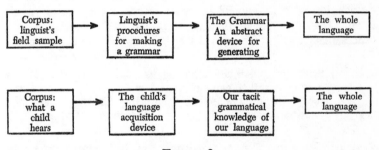

FIGURE 2

Given the present state of psychology and physiology, we certainly have little idea of what goes on in the second and third boxes, which represent what goes on in the ordinary language learner. These may be viewed as "black boxes": one cannot look inside them but one can try to describe, in abstract terms, what must be going on inside them given their inputs and outputs. The problem of linguistic theory, in a sense, is to specify the contents of the third box in the first row in such a way that we know as much as we can about what goes in the third box (and second box) of the second row.

What goes into the third box in the first row are grammatical rules, formulated in such a way that they abstractly specify a kind of machine, a sort of device for generating all and only the grammatical sentences of a language. Hence I return to the question of formulation, a question which was first raised about the structuralist attempt to describe a corpus through a "grammar of lists."

II. III   Formulation: what does a grammar look like?

The question of formulation, which we raised about the structuralist description of a corpus (or set of Scrabble® game moves), is this: after listing the alphabet and vocabulary of the corpus (or game), the structuralist is supposed to indicate what items occur with some but not other items, but how is that occurrence supposed to be indicated? Note that this question leads into another: *what sort of device is specified in an adequate description of a language?* In other words, we grant (F), following the argument of the last section that the (infinite) sentences that constitute a human language cannot be enumerated:

> [F] Syntactic investigation has as its goal the construction of a grammar that can be viewed as a device of some sort for producing [generating] the sentences of the language under analysis.   (*Syntactic Structures*, p. 11)

And, consequently, we must ask what such a construction will amount to and how it will work.

The first point about the device is that our basic concern is with (as a computer engineer might put it) *software*, not *hardware*. Transformational-generative grammarians are not interested in actually building such a device, in putting circuitry and metal together. Rather, they want to give an *abstract* description of how the device functions, of the (software) program of operations that the device follows from input to output, from start to stop.

For example, the following would be a software description of a device that would generate an infinite number of strings of symbols that just consist of a's:

(I) $S \rightarrow a + (S)$

Let me explain how we are to interpret (I). (I) is a *rule*; specifically, it is a *rewrite*, or *phrase-structure*, *rule*. The arrow means "rewrite S as $a + (S)$." S is the *initial* symbol, or input; the parentheses around the second S—(S)—mean that that part of the rewrite, as opposed to the *a*, is *optional*. Capitals are *nonterminal* symbols in that they are not found in the output, or the final line of a *derivation* that uses the rules to produce the string of symbols, or sentences, of our minilanguage. The small letters, such as *a*, are *terminal* symbols; they do not appear on the lefthand side of rewrite arrows, and when nothing but such symbols remain, the derivation of a sentence is complete.

But this explanation will be clearer through examples. Illustrations (18) and (19) show the steps, in abstract, that a device following rule (I) would go through in generating a sentence:

(18)	S	(i)	"start"
	$a + S$	(ii)	
	$a + a$	(iii)	"stop"
(19)	S	(i)	
	$a + S$	(ii)	
	$a + a + S$	(iii)	
	$a + a + a + S$	(iv)	
	$a + a + a + a$	(v)	

We now have, in software terms, the specifications of a device that will generate an infinite number of strings such as *a*, *aa*, *aaa*, *aaaa*, *aaaaa*, and so on. Each line of these derivations can be considered a *state* of the rewrite device, or software machine, that is here described—except for the last line which is the final output. Since, as inspection will show one, the line just before the final output needs to be as long as the output string, and since we have set no finite length for our "language's sentences," our device may be called an infinite-state machine.

The language we are considering is not, however, best described as a rewrite, phrase-structure, or infinite-state-machine language. The reason is that this language can be produced by a simpler device: a device which is called a *finite-state machine* and one which is presented in the "state diagram" of Figure 3.

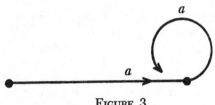

FIGURE 3

Given such a state diagram, we generate a sentence by tracing
a path from the initial dot on the left, following the arrows, to
the final dot on the left (producing a symbol at each transition
from dot [or state] to dot [or state]). Our finite-state machine
generates sentences from left to right: in moving from its first
to second state it generates an *a*; when in its second state, it has
the option (represented by the loop) of stopping or "looping-
around" for another *a and* a return to its second state, with the
same options. (The rule that this machine follows cannot be
formulated as a rewrite, or phrase structure, rule *because nothing
gets rewritten*: there are no nonterminal symbols in that each *a*
the finite-state machine produces is part of the sentence it has
generated when it stops.)

If we (somehow!) happened to meet up with a black box that
went about printing out the sentences of the very simple language we are now considering, we would not know whether
it was a finite-state machine (with recursive loops), a rewrite
machine, or some more complicated device (we would know
that it could not be a finite-state machine *without* loops). More
complicated languages, including English and other human languages, would reveal a great deal more about the internal software
of a black box that generated them. It will become clear in the
next chapter that Chomsky has demonstrated that English (and
similarly for other human languages) cannot be generated by
a finite-state machine, with or without loops, and that, further,
it cannot be generated by a rewrite machine (unless some
extremely implausible assumptions are made). Since we, aside
from our other talents, seem to be able to go about generating
the sentences of English, the implication is that our "internal
software" must have more powerful generative capacities than
those of finite-state and rewrite machines. According to Chom-

sky, a device that generates the sentences of the English language must also make use of *transformational rules.*

This will be brought out in detail in the next chapter. But the basic point about formulation may be put now. On page 37 I wrote: "After listing the alphabet and vocabulary of the games (or corpus), we are supposed to indicate what items occur with some, but not with other, items: but how is that occurrence supposed to be indicated?" The answer is: through the software description of a generative device that is general, explicit, and completely formal.

The description will be *general* in that linguists will not describe each language (whether artificial or natural) in itself by whatever rules happen to come to mind. Rather, the theory of abstract generative devices will lay out general levels of complexity in generative devices—for example, finite-state machine without loops, finite-state machine with loops, rewrite machine, and so on. And each language will be described by indicating what *general* sort of generative device is required and by specifying the particular language in the *general notation* used for describing software generative devices of that sort of generative capacity. Thus one is able to group languages in terms of the kinds of rules, or generative processes, that they require. The description will be *explicit* in that every operation that the generative device goes through in generating strings of symbols, or sentences, will be indicated in explicit detail. As a result, it will always be clear which sentences the device will generate and which it will not (one of Chomsky's complaints about traditional and structuralist grammars was that such grammars failed to be clear about this—because these linguists lacked either the means or inclination to be explicit). Finally and similarly, the description will be *formal* in a mathematical or logical sense. In generating a sentence the generative device will operate in the same way that a mathematician might prove a theorem of geometry from a given set of axioms by means of a small number of rules of inference (the process of generating a sentence and that of proving a geometric theorem are both often called derivations; it is no accident that Chomsky's first journal publication, "Systems of syntactic analysis," appeared in the *Journal of Symbolic Logic*).

Thus the way in which grammars "indicate what items occur with some, but not with other, items" is by generally, explicitly, and formally generating all sentences in which certain items so occur with "some" items *and by not generating* any sentences in which these items might occur with the "other" items. For example, the fact that *with* occurs in the context *played——her* but *of* does not, will be indicated, in a generative grammar of English, by the fact that the rules can generate the phrase *played with her* but can not generate the phrase *played of her.* One undisputed achievement of Chomsky's is that he has introduced a generation of linguists to new standards of generality, explicitness, and formality in the writing of grammars, or in the describing of languages.

This generality, explicitness, and formality have also made it much easier to show that particular candidates for the grammar of English are inadequate because they generate sentences that ordinary speakers intuitively feel are ungrammatical or because they fail to generate sentences that ordinary speakers feel are grammatical. Chomsky's work has shown that it is no easy task to construct a grammar that is *adequate,* or *observationally adequate,* in this sense (observationally adequate in that such a grammar generates all and only the observable sentences, or strings of words, that constitute English). In fact, no transformational-generative grammar of English (or any other language) has yet been constructed that completely meets the test of observational adequacy. But, though there are problem areas and though the task has come to seem somewhat more complicated than Chomsky seems to have believed when he wrote *Syntactic Structures,* linguists would now seem within reasonable distance of an observationally adequate English grammar.

Traditional and structuralist grammars, on the other hand, have tended to be idiosyncratic, implicit, and informal. Generally speaking, they have been imprecise and vague enough so that one would have difficulty, in many instances, saying whether they succeeded or failed in passing the test of observational adequacy. In the case of traditional grammars the failure came not so much in principle as in the lack of the technical means (which Chomsky in part invented and in part adapted from recent studies of abstract computing devices). With a structuralist, such as Zellig Harris, however, the principal objection was that the construction of such a device went beyond the task of "descriptive linguistics," which was to identify and categorize items in an observed (and therefore necessarily finite) corpus of utterances.

But while a structuralist might object that in principle he was analyzing a corpus and not constructing a generative device, Chomsky showed that structuralist *practice,* in segmenting the utterances of a corpus at various levels, implied a certain kind of generative device or at least a certain kind of rule—in particular, a phrase-structure device employing rewrite rules. I want to conclude this chapter by explaining this claim of Chomsky's. This will provide a provisional answer to the last of the four questions I raised on page 37: the question of how many levels there should be in an adequate description of a corpus (or a language) and how we are to tell what the correct breakup into segments is at each of these levels.

II.IV *Adequacy: How de we determine levels and segmentation in an adequate grammar?*

Consider once more Figure 1 on page 36.

Assume, for the moment, something that is not quite true, namely, that the concatenation marks (the "+" marks) at the word and phonemic levels represent actual pauses between sounds (assuming that the pauses between words are longer than those within words). Under this assumption, there is something physical and measurable that corresponds to the concatenation marks in our notation (similarly, the structuralist may identify an utterance as a series of sounds bounded by silence at either end). But we still have to account for the concatenation marks at the phrase level.

We all intuitively feel that there *is* phrase-level bracketing in sentences—there is, in other words, an intuitive sense among speakers of English that the words of the sentence of Figure 1 break up into groups in the manner indicated. For example, one feels that *father* belongs more with *my* than with *loves,* that it would be unnatural to group *old* with *loves* rather than with *men and women.* Would it not be strange, that is, to break the sentence up as *my—father loves old—men and women* rather than in the diagrammed way?

In traditional grammar, our intuitive feeling about bracketing would be expressed by labeling phrases and indicating what sorts of words could constitute them. Thus, *my father* would be labeled *Noun Phrase* or *NP*; *old men and women* would be labeled *Direct Object* (though it would also be an *NP* in that these words might also be placed at the beginning of a sentence); and *loves* would be labeled *Verb* (the whole phrase *loves old men and women* being the *Verb Phrase* or *VP*). Whether traditional, structural, or transformational-generative, any linguist will allow that a full description of a language will involve categorizing words into groups in terms of how they may form phrases, the phrases themselves being defined in terms of their capacity to combine in various ways. In terms of his generative approach Chomsky has found a way of combining the answer to two questions: (1) what is the rationale and justification for bracketing for "structural descriptions" of sentences? and (2) what sort of device will generate English sentences? When we lay out the software device that will generate English sentences (as strings of words), we find that the derivation steps (as in [18] and [19] provide the categorizing and bracketing that both traditional and structural linguists often found arbitrary and indeterminate.

For example, consider the following group of rules (as purely illustrative, for they leave out many features of English syntax):

(20)   i)   Sentence → NP + VP
      ii)   NP → (D) + N
     iii)   VP → Verb + NP
      iv)   D → my, their, the, etc.
       v)   N → father, mother, etc.
      vi)   Verb → loves, hates, etc.

Now we can generate the derivation (one which is general, explicit, and formal):

(21)   sentence   (i)
      NP + VP   (ii)
      D + N + VP   (iii)
      D + N + Verb + NP   (iv)

my + N + Verb + NP	(v)
my + father + Verb + NP	(vi)
my + father + loves + NP	(vii)
my + father + loves + N	(viii)
my + father + loves + old men and women	(ix)

By following the rewrite rules of (20), we have generated the derivation (21). One sees that exactly the same sentence could be generated, with a different set of steps in the derivation, by following the rules in a different order. I have not specified any particular order for the rules because so long as the same final string is produced, the order of application does not contribute to the bracketing, or structural description, that the sentence has for a speaker of English. Whatever the order of application, the same bracketing, or tree diagram, is generated: in this case, the bracketing and "upside down tree" of Figure 1. Hence we can call either the bracketing or the tree diagram *the structural description* of the sentence if we provide labels for the nonterminal categories as in Figure 4, while (21) is just one derivation among several, each providing the basis for the same structural description.

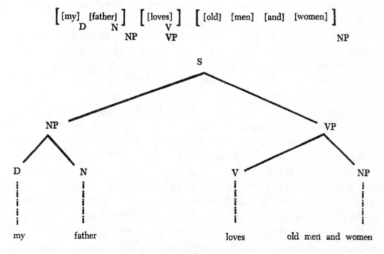

FIGURE 4

Of course, the sentence could be generated in ways that would not provide such structural descriptions (or provide ones that do not reflect the ordinary speaker's intuitions about structure). For example, the following finite-state diagram, Figure 5, would also generate the sentence but without the structural description, while a different set of rewrite rules might generate the sentence with an entirely different structural description.

FIGURE 5

Since the structuralists did think that sentences could be segmented at successively higher levels of analysis (phonemic, word, and phrase-structure levels), and since each level seemed to be just further combinations of the material of the level below, it was natural to interpret the structural linguists as *implicitly* maintaining that a rewrite, or phrase-structure, device was sufficient for English syntax. Thus what happens in effect in proceeding from higher to lower levels is that a symbol is rewritten as one or more symbols, eventuating in a string of terminal symbols—the observed sentence. In other words, so Chomsky reasoned, were a structuralist to recognize that since a natural language could not be given by enumeration, it must be described through specifying a generative device, then the structuralist would realize that his methods of analysis implied that the device would be a rewrite, or phrase-structure, device. Still other sorts of rules—phonological rules—would be involved in converting the output of the generative device, which would be strings of words (or, more strictly, morphemes), into the specific sounds and rhythms of articulate speech. These phonological rules, which structuralists called *morphophonemic* in that they converted strings of morphemes into phonemic structures, would also be, in a structuralist grammar, rewrite rules though of a slightly different sort; however, since Chomsky's most exciting early work was in syntax, not phonology, I will not have anything to say about phonology for some pages.

But the general point is simple. What distinguishes phonemic and word (morphemic) levels of grammatical analysis are different kinds of rules, in effect different components of a generative grammatical device; similarly the phrase-structure bracketing of sentences is seen as a natural product of the simplest and most revealing set of general, explicit, and formal rules that are capable of generating the sentences of the language in question. An adequate grammar, as Chomsky has put it, must—as a general, explicit, and formal generative device—meet both the standard of *observational* adequacy and the standard of *descriptive* adequacy. That is, it must have both a "weak" and a "strong" generative capacity of the right sort. It meets observational adequacy by its weak generative capacity of producing all and only those strings of words that ordinary speakers intuitively recognize as grammatical. It meets descriptive adequacy by its strong generative capacity of producing such grammatical strings in a way that provides structural descriptions (trees, bracketings, etc.) which ordinary speakers find intuitively acceptable. We might put these points in a slightly revised version of (F).

> (F1) "Syntactic investigation has as its goal the construction of a grammar that can be viewed as a device" that meets observational adequacy through its weak generation of all and only those strings of words that ordinary speakers find intuitively grammatical, and meets descriptive adequacy, at the same time, through its strong generation of structural descriptions for those strings that are similarly acceptable to ordinary speakers.

We might add that Chomsky wants generative grammars to approach the goal of *explanatory* adequacy. This goal is approached in linguistic theory by relating the linguist's procedures, in writing observationally and descriptively adequate grammars of particular languages, to hypotheses about the (software) structure of a child's "language-acquisition device." That is, by making the natural assumption that a child is equally capable of learning whatever human language he happens to be exposed to and of learning its infinite character through exposure to a relatively small number of actual sentences, one would expect a certain uniformity in the structure of grammars of all human languages (this *uniformity* constituting a definition of *human language*). Explanatory adequacy is reached when the specific means by which the grammar of a particular language reaches observational and descriptive adequacy is *explained* (or justified) in terms of a general theory of human language that specifies the child's language-acquisition device. As in Figure 2, page 53, the linguist's procedures for making observationally and descriptively adequate grammars should be further restricted and made uniform by theorizing about the kind of (software) device that would most efficiently and economically generate the grammar of any human language to which it was given some limited exposure.

Again, it should be emphasized that Chomsky still envisions a line between specifically linguistic and psychological and physiological questions. A psychologist, or neurophysiologist, might investigate the actual "hardware" through which language is learned or generated, and also study the interaction between man's pure capacity to acquire language and generate sentences (i.e., play the Scrabble® word game) and man's many other intellectual abilities. But the linguist is essentially concerned with just linguistic competence, with, that is, software devices capable of strongly generating the sentences of particular natural languages, devices whose general internal structure would be regulated and explained by theory about the "software" of the device capable of producing such particular grammars from limited exposure to sentences of particular natural languages. The crucial question is whether the transformational-generative linguist can give a specification of linguistic competence of the software of a competent speaker that is detailed enough to guide, and be tested by, the more straightforward laboratory work of psychologists and physiologists. Can the linguist tell us much about the "black box" of the human mind?

III *Summary*

Chomsky started with the structuralist assumption that a language is (just) a set of structurally described sentences that happen to occur in a single speech community at a particular time (A-D). The structuralist insists that he, as a good behaviorist, studies what people *do* (what series of noises they actually make, a corpus), not what they think they are doing; further, distinguishing linguistics from behavioral psychology proper, the structuralist insists on just considering *noise*, not the generating source of the noise. But, given that a human language has an infinite number of sentences (E), and, hence, that enumeration and analysis of a corpus can neither amount to description of a language nor be related to such a description by straightforward probabilities, Chomsky concludes that neither a corpus nor its language can be described except through the general, explicit, and formal specification of a generative device that meets goals of observational, descriptive, and explanatory adequacy (F1). In other words, the question of procedure and projection led to new views about formulation and adequacy. And the taxonomic view of linguistics and language, when subject to internal criticism, led to a generative viewpoint. A viewpoint that might make possible, by means of the specification of linguistic competence in the form of a software generative device, some substantial linguistic contribution to the study of the human mind. (In the next chapter it will be seen that even if structuralist analytic practice were interpreted as a view to the effect that human languages are phrase-structure-rule languages, that is, languages that could be generated by rewrite devices, such a view would still be inadequate.)

It may be helpful to run through Chomsky's general critique of structuralism in another way. The argument of the last paragraph is sometimes put by Chomsky as a methodological point in a vocabulary adapted in part from mathematical logic. Mathematical logicians, when they consider procedures for solving problems or constructing proofs, effectively distinguish, when considering bodies of propositions (or mathematical "languages"), the following questions: (1) Whether there is a mechanical, step-by-step procedure for *discovering* proofs. (2) Whether there is a mechanical, step-by-step procedure for *deciding* that particular propositions have proofs (or do not), leaving aside the question of how these proofs may be discovered (often both (1) and (2) come to the same thing in artificial

languages—*decidability*). (3) Whether it can at least be established that every proposition (that can be formulated in the
mathematical language) can be proved, *or* its denial can be
assumed without inconsistency, though one might not be able
to arrive at the proof of any mechanical procedure (systems
in which everything that must be true is also provable are called
complete). (4) Whether, given that (1) and (2) do not obtain,
it is at least possible to evaluate partially completed solutions,
in other words, to establish mechanically that one "solution"
is consistent with what is assumed in a way that another is not,
without determining that the preferred "solution" is *the* solution
(for example, we may *evaluate* one grammar as more consistent
with the data than another without knowing that the preferred
grammar is *the* grammar, the provable solution—there may be
better solutions and more data).

As Chomsky puts it in *Syntactic Structures*, given a corpus
of utterances belonging to a natural language, there is neither
a *discovery* nor a *decision procedure*. That is, given a particular
corpus (or set of assumptions) belonging to a natural language,
there is no mechanical, step-by-step procedure for discovering
the grammar of the language. If there were such a discovery
procedure, structuralism would be vindicated, because this would
mean that each corpus of noise could be *adequately and de-
terminately* described. Even if there were a decision procedure
this implication would hold, though it would require creativity
for the linguist to arrive at *the* grammar.

Chomsky's claim that there is no discovery or decision procedure for arriving at *the* grammar of a language, although grammars may be given comparative evaluations, is a way of pointing
out that it is impossible to write *the* grammars of human languages without a very substantial theory of the human mind and
its language acquiring, and processing, software. Presumably,
Chomsky would accept the claim that adequate and determinate
grammars are possible only if such a substantial theory is part
of the input for arriving at such grammars. There must be a
number of universal features common to the grammars of all
natural languages, and these must derive from innate features
of man's language-acquisition device, in order for there to be
adequately determinate grammars (that is, by rough analogy,

for *completeness* to obtain, regarding the grammar of each language as what may be "proved" from sentences of that language *plus* the "axioms" of a more substantial theory of language and language acquisition than we now have).

Linguists can only go about determining the universal characteristics of human language in an indirect and conjectural way, of course: there is no direct way of looking into the "black box" of language processing and acquisition. As linguists proceed, in painstaking and piecemeal fashion, to construct and evaluate general, explicit, and formal grammars, or partial grammars, of particular languages, it may be hoped that they will find universal features and thus that they will approach explanatory adequacy. For an analogy, imagine that we wanted to know about the internal structure of some kind of computer found on Mars: the rules of the game are that we cannot look inside at the hardware but can only try to infer the inner structure through observing the inputs and outputs. What we note is that when one of these machines is exposed to a small number of strings (drawn, apparently, from a particular infinite set of strings, a "language") its output is, more or less, the infinite set. We can see that it is impossible, using just logic principles, to arrive at the infinite output by taking a typical input (i.e., no discovery or decision procedure exists). All we can say is that, given a particular input, such and such an output (as generated by a grammar) is more likely than some other sort. As we write partial grammars of outputs A through Z, for inputs A through Z, we would expect various uniformities, and we would reformulate our grammars in terms of these uniformities. The internal software of these Martian computers will be, in particular, the assumptions that must be made in order to get in a regular fashion from these various inputs to their respective outputs.

It is to the degree that the writing of particular grammars must depend on evaluation and creative guess that the goal of explanatory adequacy becomes crucial.

It is easy enough to see how intriguing this approach might be. The greatest, earliest, and most pervasive of man's intellectual achievements is language. Children could be said without exaggeration to perform their first and most marvelous computative feat in moving from a relatively small input of utterances, and not much guidance (usually), to a general knowledge of how to speak and understand their native language. One might even speculate that conscious thought and reasoning, as we characteristically experience it, is something that *follows after* the acquisition of language. The question is whether Chomsky's indirect approach can produce substantial results, can tell us something reasonably specific about a crucial portion of our internal software, particularly insofar as it might suggest something, however indirectly, about the actual hardware that could be the physical basis for the fundamental software.

The most crucial question before us is thus the one with which I ended the Introduction. Though he is concerned with man's linguistic abilities more particularly, Chomsky, like Freud, wants to find out something about the inner, essentially unconscious, structure of the mind—and not through direct neurophysiological investigation but through postulating structures that underlie and explain the complicated human activity that we can look at directly. The issue is whether those linguists who follow Chomsky's lead will be able to develop theories that are sufficiently justified on linguistic terms and suggestive and determinate enough to help psychophysiological research and to be tested by it. To some degree I think Chomsky has been vindicated, as I will try to show. But there have been disappointments and serious problems have cropped up.

It should be obvious by now that Chomsky's rationalism—his revival of the notion of universal grammar and innate ideas, and his claim that psychology has to make use of mentalistic concepts—can be thought of as a natural outgrowth of his linguistic work. To maintain that human beings have built into them language acquisition devices of considerable complexity is to maintain something like a modern version of the doctrine of innate ideas. The notion that the generative devices that are the grammars of the thousands of human languages may happen to have a very considerable number of common properties is *something* like the notion of universal grammar maintained by seventeenth-century rationalists. The mentalistic claim that it is, at least for the immediate future, inevitable and profitable for linguists and psychologists to study the software that is the mind, rather than confining themselves to observed physical behavior and dim hopes about brain physiology, is a claim that grants provisional support to traditional rationalist views about the importance and independence of the mind. The justice of these comparisons, and of the general philosophic viewpoint that one might associate with Chomsky, is a matter that I will take up in chapter 4.

Again, the justice of my ambitious (and ambiguous) comparison between Chomsky's and Einstein's revolutions will be taken firmly in hand in subsequent passages. But brief reminders now seem in order. Both Einstein and Chomsky criticized a prevailing scientific view that insisted that a subject matter (space, time, etc., in one case, utterance in the other) might be adequately characterized without taking into account the observer (speaker-hearer); both added a dimension to the subject matter of their discipline that suggested a very different general view of underlying reality but which did not directly challenge much of the observational data of the older view. It belongs to the next chapter to display more fully the new technical apparatus that made it possible for Chomsky to explain his new views and to suggest that structuralism (specifically the implicit commitment to phrase-structure grammars) can appear as a fairly arbitrary special case, rather than the only possible view; I will there make the case for regarding transformational-generative linguistics as having been supported by relatively delicate crucial tests. I hardly need to add that Chomsky's work has been seen as having all sorts of sweeping implications for everything from the genetic basis of language learning to the politics of the United States intervention in Vietnam; the attacks on both Chomskyan specifics and generalities have been equally sweeping.

One small note before we go on to a more detailed consideration of kinds of generative devices. The reader may have wondered at the fact that I have treated *old men and women* as lacking internal structure, as if it were a simple noun like *father*. In fact, of course, traditional, structural, or transformational linguists would want to say that *old men and women* is not an indivisible syntactical unit and does have internal structure. In what way should this phrase be bracketed?

Many people immediately see that this phrase can be heard
or understood in two ways. The father in question loves "men
who are old" *and* "women who are old"; or the father in question
loves "men who are old" *and* "women (in general)." That is,
in terms of brackets, there are two possibilities:

(22) old (men and women)

(23) (old men) and (women)

Despite that when someone actually says the sentence either
the context or the emphasis and pauses may make it obvious
whether (22) or (23) is meant, the sentence as a string of
words is *ambiguous*. Not only is the sentence ambiguous but
its ambiguity can come out in its *bracketing*. The words themselves—*old*, *men*, *women*, *and*—are not individually ambiguous:
the ambiguity is in the structural description of the sentence
of which these words are terminal elements. The sentence would
still be ambiguous if we substituted other nouns and adjectives:
*fat foxes and rabbits, tired horses and camels, stupid dingbats
and hard hats*, and so on for any string of the form $Adj. + N +
and + N$. This adds a dimension to the notion of structural
description. The structural description, which is given through
the strong generative capacity of a grammatical device, should
account for *structural ambiguity*. It should, that is, provide as
many different structural descriptions of a sentence as there are
different structurally ambiguous readings of the sentence.

But it is rather cumbersome to account for this ambiguity, or
this sentence for that matter, within a rewrite, or phrase-structure, grammar. Why? Obviously, we could have rules that would
allow us to break down NP into $Adj. + NP^1$ and NP^1 into $NP^2 +
and + NP^2$, which in turn would become $Adj. + (N + and + N)$;
and other rules that would take NP into $NP^3 + and + NP^3$ and
thence to $(Adj. + N) + and + N$. But this would be cumbersome: it would be neater intuitively, since the same sort of
maneuver seems involved, to have one rule of conjunction.

Further, exactly the same process of conjunction seems to
go on generally, not just with nouns, for example, *she played
and danced vigorously, they are adding and subtracting numbers, he types quickly and accurately*. We have, in effect, the

following situation. If S_1 and S_2 are grammatical sentences, with S_1 differing from S_2 only in that Y appears in S_1 where Z appears in S_2; and Y and Z are constituents of the same type (both *VP*'s, *NP*'s, etc.); then the result of replacing Y by $Y + and + Z$ will be a grammatical sentence, S_3.

We could indicate this, in our grammar, by means of one simple and very general rule:

(24) $U + Y + W; \ U + Z + W \rightarrow U + Y + and + Z + W$

In this rule U and W are (terminal) strings of words and Y and Z are (nonterminal) elements of the same sort (*NP*'s, *VP*'s, etc.). But this rule is not at all a rewrite or phrase-structure rule. A rewrite rule is one that "rewrites" *one symbol* as one or more symbols, that is, it descends from *one node* of a *tree*, rewriting that node as one or more symbols (ignoring the rest of the structure). But (24) deletes and rearranges several symbols; it has two sentences, with structural descriptions, as input, rather than one symbol. Generically, (24) is a transformational rule. We shall see in the next chapter in greater detail how Chomsky developed the argument that English is a transformational-rule language, not just a phrase-structure-rule language (as are most artificial languages), let alone a still simpler finite-state-rule language.

CHAPTER 2

Three Sorts of Generative Devices

TO describe a language as a linguist, then, is to specify the software of a device that will generate the strings of terminal symbols (words) that are the sentences of the language and, at the same time, to provide a structural description of these sentences. Doing this is part of specifying competence in a particular language; it is not specifying the complicated mixture of linguistic and nonlinguistic talents that people call upon in actual conversation nor is it indicating the actual character of the hardware employed. Recalling the Scrabble® Sentence Cube Game, our problem is to specify a device that will generate all and only the moves that might be made, given the (terminal) vocabulary of English, plus the nonterminal vocabulary of syntactical categories (*VP, NP, N, Adj.*, and so on), and a set of rules. Whatever our linguistic hardware is it cannot be *simpler*, or less powerful, than that of the simplest device that can generate (and thus structurally describe) these sentences. The investigation will not tell us what human linguistic hardware actually is; but it will tell us, in a general sort of way, what the mind *must* be powerful enough to do—just as *any* computing machine that can add numbers must be capable of certain extremely simple operations, however complex its actual hardware may be.

I *Finite-State Grammars*

In the last chapter I briefly described finite-state devices as those that had only a terminal vocabulary and had only a finite number of internal states. At "start" the device is in one of its finite states, then it switches to its next state by following an arrow to a box from which it randomly selects a (terminal) vocabulary item, the beginning of its output. So it proceeds, following the arrows and switching from state to state by printing out items in a string, until it reaches "stop."

There are two sorts of finite-state devices: those without "loops" that allow the device to return to a previous state, and those that have such loops. If a device lacks loops, it will soon run through all of the boxes that the arrows allow it to travel through. Hence it can generate only strings that are no longer than the number of boxes (at best). With loops, indefinitely longer sentences may be generated, but the device is still a finite-state device. Why? Because the device proceeds in exactly the same way whichever state it is in (whichever box it is approaching), *no matter what its previous states have been*—it is not part of its state to know what its previous states have been. It does not "remember," for example, how many times it has been back to a previous state by looping. If it did "remember," then it would have as many states as the number of times it could loop back (which has no definite limit and hence one would no longer have a finite-state device).

In *Syntactic Structures* Chomsky considered a finite-state device without loops that could generate two strings—*the man comes*, and *the men come*. He changed it to a finite-state device with loops by adding a loop, which provided the vocabulary item *old*, at the node after *the*, thus recursively generating *the old man comes, the old old man comes, the old old old man comes*, and so on. Another example is shown in Figure 6 (p. 74). Whether or not we ignore the loops, the device of Figure 6 has as many states (twenty-three) as boxes. If we treat it as a loopless device, the longest sentence it could generate would be eight words long: for example, *the old man has seen the old men, the old God has loved the visible worlds, these colorless men have seen my old father*. With loops, longer sentences are possible. And, of course, we can have sentences that are shorter: *the invisible God created the visible world, my father loves that colorless idea, this man created furiously*. It will also generate queer sentences which seem meaningless but which none the less are grammatical, at least by comparison with clearly ungrammatical strings. For example, the sentence *colorless green ideas sleep furiously*—which the finite-state device shown in Figure 6 generates exactly as it does the sentences *colorless old*

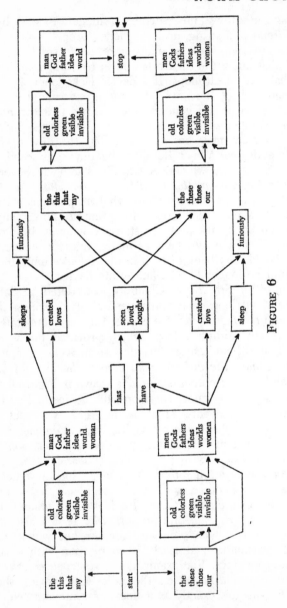

FIGURE 6

men love furiously or *the old man created furiously*—does not seem to have a meaning; but it does seem to preserve grammatical structure in a way that is not done by sentences like *furiously sleep ideas green colorless* or *colorless green idea sleep furiously* (neither of which can be generated by the finite-state device of Figure 6).

There are two crucial questions one wants to ask about finite-state grammatical devices: (1) Why might someone consider human languages to be finite state languages? That is, if English were, for example, a finite-state language, what (if anything) might this fact imply about the mental processes of people who are linguistically competent users of English? (2) What proof—in a reasonably strict sense of proof—has Chomsky provided that English and other human languages cannot be finite-state languages? But before considering these major issues there are two preliminary points that I want to make.

The first point is that we could construct a finite-state diagram—a version of the one diagrammed in Figure 6—that would provide a more restricted simulation of grammaticality. One might call Figure 6 a "liberal" grammar in that it does generate semigrammatical sentences, or what I called "queer" sentences in the second to the last paragraph. The question is, in various ways, a matter of degree. The strings *furious sleep ideas green colorless* or *green sleeps father old my* are obviously ungrammatical. And strings such as *the men come* and *the man comes* are obviously grammatical. Most of us would feel, however, some uncertainty if asked whether *colorless green ideas sleep furiously* is a full-fledged grammatical English sentence. In *Syntactic Structures* (1957) Chomsky operated under "liberal" assumptions. He was interested in devices that would generate such more-or-less grammatical, though meaningless, sentences as *colorless green ideas sleep furiously*: sentences which might be called poetic, or metaphoric, or syntactically well-formed but senseless. In *Aspects of the Theory of Syntax* (1965) Chomsky was interested in developing an improved and more powerful, but also more restricted, syntax, one which would mark *colorless green ideas sleep furiously* as ungrammatical (still more recently, Chomsky and many generative linguists have

more or less reverted to the view that this sentence is grammatical, though it is now explicitly labeled as meaningless, or
semantically malformed, by a "semantic component" that was
lacking from his first grammars).

These changes can be misunderstood. It is not so much that
linguists keep on changing their intuitions about this and similar
sentences; rather, it has been more a question of finding different
(hopefully more complete and more adequate!) ways of
capturing and explaining such intuitions in a general, explicit,
and formal manner. The reader may recall my first discussion
of the sentence (on page 31), where I made the point that it
was a borderline case. There I commented that if one wanted to
say flatly that the sentence is ungrammatical (because meaningless), one would be confronted with a range of odd, illogical,
or senseless sentences, and somewhere one would have to draw
lines. Very recent work has been much concerned with the
feasibility of drawing such lines. But—and this is the point to
remember now—this has not been a matter of distinguishing
finite-state, phrase-structure, and transformational grammars:
for practical purposes *any* of these could be formulated so as
to mark such odd sentences as grammatical *or* formulated so
as to mark them as ungrammatical.

The second preliminary point is that I could easily have added
boxes in such a way that they would generate the conjunctive
sentence I have considered at length in the previous chapter.
The device in Figure 6 now generates *my father loves old men*.
Obviously I could add another box, with *and* and similar words
in it, with a route from the second box with plural nouns that
would lead to the new "conjunction" box and back to that
second plural noun box. However, we would have to add three
other identical new boxes for each of the noun boxes. We could
not, in other words, draw routes from each of the four noun
boxes to the "conjunction" box and back again because one
might then return not to the noun box one started with but to
another, thus creating an ungrammatical string. For example,
one could then form *my father loves old men and idea* by
moving from the "conjunction" box to the second singular noun
box, not back to the second plural box. Of course, someone might
say that we could have just one "conjunction" box but write it

into the "rules" that the route should return from the "conjunction" box to the same box of origin. But that would be to go beyond the power of the general sort of device under consideration, for it would mean that the device would "remember" its previous states, the action of the device *not* being determined simply and solely by the particular state (or box) that it happened to be in. Hence we must have four boxes *or* some device essentially more powerful than a finite-state device.

Indeed, if we wished to make our finite-state device adequate so far as the use of conjunction goes, we would need many more than four boxes. Obviously, it is as natural to conjoin adjectives, verbs, and whole sentences as it is to conjoin nouns. One wants to be able to generate *that old and colorless man..., this woman has seen and loved...*, and *this woman has bought that man and that man has bought this woman.* But, again, one would need separate "conjunction" boxes to avoid the creation of ungrammatical strings; by previous reasoning something on the order of twelve boxes would be needed (and still more if we made any attempt to expand our finite-state device). Since conjunction seems to be *one* sort of process and since all of these boxes would be the same, the limitations on "memory" that define the nature of a finite-state device being all that forces these clumsy repetitions on us, this way of handling conjunction seems quite unsatisfactory. As I argued at the end of the last chapter, a phrase-structure grammar also seems to have related difficulties with conjunction.

Reflecting on this clumsiness, one wants to ask the first of the crucial questions that I mentioned. Why might someone consider English, or any language, to be a finite-state language? What would follow if the sentences that constitute English could be generated by a finite-state device (though, perhaps, a "complicated" and "clumsy" device)? Chomsky did not begin by examining finite-state grammars because linguists, structuralists specifically, were explicitly and seriously proposing that English was a finite-state language. Since structuralists accepted the linguistic reality of phrase structure and made use in effect of nonterminal symbols and rewrite rules, a full criticism of their views would mean showing that English, and other human languages, were beyond the generative power of phrase-struc-

ture grammars, not just beyond the even more restricted power
of finite-state devices.

The reason Chomsky felt the need to criticize finite-state-
device grammars of the specific sort we have been considering
is twofold: (1) Such a view of language seemed the natural
result of *information theory*, a sophisticated mathematical model
of communication that developed from World War II studies of
telecommunication systems—and which deeply impressed psychologists and linguists in the 1950's. Hence the model was a
natural candidate for consideration, and the generality and so-
phistication of the model made some feel it was the only candidate. (2) The view of language processing that was suggested
by such a model fitted well with the behaviorist preconceptions
that dominated experimental psychology through much of this
century and particularly during the 1950's. Hence this view
was one that Chomsky found natural to attack.

Still, either in conversation with Chomsky or in reading his
works, it would be hard to say to what degree Chomsky came
to oppose behaviorism because it suggested inadequate language
models and to what degree he came to oppose such models because they realized behaviorism. Some critics, who feel they
certainly must accept much of Chomsky's linguistic work but
who feel deeply committed to behaviorism, or feel that such
"philosophic" issues are somehow irrelevant, argue that Chomsky's "important and solid" contributions to knowledge come
in his early work, which they happily find unaffected by the
views about psychology that they associate with his later work.
But I think a close reading of *Syntactic Structures*, and of the
much longer unpublished work from which *Syntactic Structures*
derives, shows that Chomsky's opposition to behaviorism was
present from the start. Behind this biographical debate lies a
more crucial issue: can the contributions to linguistic theory be
clearly and cleanly separated from the views about psychology?
Can one buy the first without some commitment to the second?
Chomsky's answer, of course, is no. There is, in his view, comparatively little of interest in a study of grammar that will show
nothing whatsoever about human psychology; moreover, with
such limits, adequate grammatical characterization of a human

language simply cannot be achieved—which is the essence of Chomsky's criticism of linguistic structuralism.

Information theory began in the military concern with tele-communications: with the need to ensure accuracy, efficiency, and secrecy in communication channels, which meant balancing the need to repeat parts of messages (*redundancy*) in order to cope with distorting *noise* in the channel, against the need to be brief (since redundancy is extremely helpful to code breakers and, in any case, redundant messages are more expensive to send). In the telegraph, the earliest and simplest form of tele-communication, messages are realized simply as alternating bursts of electricity in a wire. The only choices are between power on and power off at any given moment, so the message might be diagrammed as a series of dots and blanks that make up a line moving from left to right across the page. At each point, the choice between power on and power off may be thought of as a "bit" of information, a choice between two possible pathways, and possible messages may be more fully diagrammed as a tree whose trunk branches in two, and each branch in two once more, and so on across the page. Our finite-state grammar is a development of this notion with branching represented as a choice between taking the arrowed path to one box or the other, proceeding from left to right across the page (the choice between words *within* boxes could also be repre-sented by branching but this choice is random and unstructured from the point of view of syntax, specifically in that no syn-tactical rules restrict the choice—hence one does not need to diagram it in a finite-state grammar).

Information theory assumes that *information* implies *choice* between pathways; if only one path can be taken, we gain no information when it is taken. The amount of information is proportionate to the improbability, or unpredictability, of the choice made. If there is no choice—if, for example, there is only one pathway that may be taken from one box to the next, so that the next (and completely predictable) step could be said to have a probability of 100 percent—there is redundancy, and, from the theoretical viewpoint of information theory, no informa-tion is conveyed by the step.

As we have seen, syntax has nothing to do with probability of occurrence. Many syntactically malformed strings of words do occur with some frequency and many perfectly well-formed sentences have a vanishingly small chance of occurrence. As Chomsky interpreted the information theoretic viewpoint in *Syntactic Structures*, the information, or meaning, of a sentence message would be determined by the various improbabilities associated with each "choice" of a new state in the finite-state device. But syntax, or grammaticality in the strict sense, would have nothing to do with such probabilities. Syntax, as displayed in a finite-state device, would simply indicate what steps, and so what sentences, are possible, whatever their probability. Our grammatical device cannot "choose" ungrammatical strings; hence no information is produced by its generation of any grammatical, as opposed to any ungrammatical, string. The finite-state syntactical device would, that is, lay down the framework of possibilities within which probabilities might be determined.

We now have before us the rudiments of a theoretic model of linguistic production and understanding. It would seem to suggest something about the psychology of language use. Though Chomsky has little to say in detail about how such a model might be suggestive in this way, there are some obvious possibilities.

Consider, first, what the model might suggest about how people hear, or hear and understand, sentences. Leaving aside the conversion of sounds into words, contextual clues, and so on, one might imagine the hearer taking in the first word of the sentence (among all the words which his knowledge of syntax tells him might begin a sentence). His syntactical knowledge now tells him that various words are possible second choices, and his semantic knowledge assigns various "information weightings" to these possible choices. The second word is heard and the process continues. In those cases where there is no choice, his linguistic knowledge, his "internalized" finite-state device, will lead him to expect and hear the only possible continuation. Equally, if the hearer's sense of probabilities makes only one continuation of the sentence at all probable, the hearer's semantic knowledge allows him to infer, to leap ahead to the end of the sentence. Of course, little of this is a conscious, or clearly conscious, process, any more than most of the complicated maneuvers of daily cognitive life, and this fact does make the use of words like *knowledge* and *infer* subject to criticism, but I will defer a direct and full consideration of this issue until the next chapter. Certainly people do have expectations as they hear sentences, in the sense that they may be very startled by the frustration of their expectations in plays on words, errors, and so on, though they are not conscious of these expectations until and unless they are frustrated.

So far as the speaker's construction of sentences goes, this sort of model might suggest a somewhat different treatment. While this suggestion might be discounted in the case of the hearer, it is not easy to resist the feeling that a speaker often (always?) has "something in mind" that he wants to say before he starts to construct a specific sentence—"something in mind" that will affect the manner of sentence construction. Whether our scruples are correct or not is not an easy question to answer.

But we can set this question aside in that we might simply imagine our speaker playing the Scrabble® word game. In such a case we could think of him as selecting any first word (that could begin a sentence), then selecting one of the possible second steps, and so on. His ability to construct English sentences (without concern with meaning, use in particular social situations, and so on) could then, one might hope, be represented generatively by a finite-state syntactical device. As one went on to consider all the semantic, contextual, and other factors that enter into everyday speech situations, these factors might be though of as interacting with this basic syntactical ability, with an intellectual capacity that could be explained as an internalization of the finite-state device. Were English a finite state language (that is, one whose sentences could be generated by a finite-state device), then someone who exhibits a basic grammatical grasp of the language, whether in the multifaceted situations of everyday language use or in the simple game situation, could be said to have the finite-state "software" in question.

How this "software" is realized in the actual "hardware" of the brain is another question. But knowing what the "software" is will help guide the investigation of the physiological "hardware." Indeed, it would seem as silly to investigate the brain's enormously complicated neurological "hardware" without a very good idea of its functioning "software" as it would be to try to understand the innards of an electronic computer without knowing any logic or mathematics. It would be sillier, in fact, because computers are in no way as miniaturized and as adaptable as the human brain.

One notes that so far as syntactical knowledge alone goes, one might not need separate models for speaker and hearer. In both situations we would seem to make use of the same knowledge, the same linguistic competence. Throughout his work Chomsky has stuck to this "neutrality" between speaker's and hearer's syntactical knowledge. The factors of actual *speech performance* are conceived as additions to this core of grammatical knowledge. But in three respects finite-state grammars, with or without recursive "loops," differ from Chomsky's other, more powerful, models. First, sentences are generated "left to right": first word, second word, and so on to the final word. Secondly, there are no nonterminal symbols involved, which means in effect that the device provides no structural descriptions of sentences, and, presumably, it also means that such parsing belongs outside the knowledge of the ordinary competent speaker. Thirdly, the device is finite-state, having as many internal states as it has boxes.

Such devices have a great deal of simplicity and they lend themselves to information-theoretic-characterization in the way that has been sketched. By being relatively simple they also have an appeal to the behaviorist.

Though behaviorism is a loose collection of partially related views rather than a fixed position, one point on which any behaviorist would agree is that human psychology should fix upon an unprejudiced description of human behavior, particularly a study of how, and within what limits, "programs of reinforcement" (to use B. F. Skinner's favored vocabulary) will change behavior, or "teach" new behavior, in much the same general sort of way that it will affect animals whose perceptual apparatus is at least relatively similar to man's. In all respects possible, the postulating of any sort of complicated, abstract, internal processes is to be avoided, certainly insofar as such talk cannot be reformulated in purely behavioral terms. Behaviorism, that is, is opposed to mentalism. The ideal description, from such a behaviorist viewpoint, is one which characterizes the experimental subject in "stimulus-response" terms. Such and such a stimulus will be followed by such and such a behavioral response; more fully, such and such a "program of reinforcement" for spontaneous behavior will put the experimental subject in a condition such that new stimulus-response sequences are "learned." The ideal, in other words, is *control* and *predictability*. The psychologist "understands" a form of behavior if he is able to control it, that is, to reinforce or eradicate it.

But finite-state syntactical devices have more specific attractive features for the behaviorist than simplicity. The left to right generation of sentences appeals because it suggests that one might think of the first word as a stimulus which past experience (past "programs of reinforcement") causes the "subject" to "respond" by expecting, or adopting, various second words, and so on. If a grammar indicates only one path, the stimulus could be said to lead to one fixed response, whereas if there is more than one path, this might be regarded as a complex, weighted response. For an animal example, one might distinguish the simple case in which a rat has learned that only one particular path will get him through a maze, and so uniformly responds by taking that path, from a complex case where the rat may have learned that a left turn works a bit better than a right turn, and both work better than a straight path, though all three have some probability of working.

The lack of nonterminal symbols is similarly suggestive. Whether one regards each word (each state) as a stimulus that leads, with weighted probabilities, to a response, or at a more general level regards the string of words as a response to situational stimuli, there is no suggestion of mentalistic states, or abstractions, *that are not realized in explicit sensory events*, that is, in what is heard or characterized in terms of observed behavior. If English is a finite-state language, it will be reasonable to suppose that the ordinary competent speaker-hearer of English need have nothing more stored in his thinking apparatus than particular words that he has actually heard or seen and various associations between them which are also derived from sequences that he has actually heard or seen.

This point may well remind one of the general empiricist tradition from which behaviorism derived. An eighteenth-century empiricist like David Hume maintained that our ideas were essentially copies, or manipulated memories, of our sensory experiences, as opposed to the rationalists who maintained that the human mind was not so much a passive receiver of sensations, which it could copy and assemble by the simple process of association, as a complicated and active structure with innate tendencies to develop various abstract ideas that could not at all be identified with particular associations of experience (could not be identified, that is, with what is, or can be, seen or heard or otherwise sensed, such as terminal symbols).

Of course, this whole traditional debate about ideas between empiricists and rationalists has been criticized as too fuzzy to allow hopes for a very clear solution, or experimental or logical resolution; and the debate has subdivided in various ways since the eighteenth century. But it is not hard to see that Chomsky has found a way of narrowing the issue. If it can be shown that a generative device that can generate the sentences of English (considered for the moment just as strings of words) must employ nonterminal symbols, then this suggests some credit for the rationalist position—within, one must remember, this particular way of narrowing the issue.

By *nonterminal symbol* I have in mind, of course, terms such as *Verb, NP, VP*, which I introduced in discussing phrase structure, or rewrite, grammars. These were nonterminal in the sense that they did not appear in the sentences generated by such grammars—the derivation of a sentence is incomplete if any nonterminal symbols remain. Of course these symbols do occur in the sentences that grammarians construct *when they write about languages*; they are not, in that sense, nonterminal symbols in the grammarian's language, as opposed to the language he writes about.

But the point about mentalism, about the need for ideas that are not at all directly realized in experience, still remains. It remains because someone may have an essentially adequate grasp of English without knowing the grammarian's technical terminology. There is a clear sense in which such an individual can be said to internalize a knowledge of these grammatical notions though he has no name for them (that is, he has no terminal symbol for them available). He can be said to internalize these notions if English is (at least) a phrase-structure-rule, or rewrite-rule, language. Though we shall have a definite proof of this shortly, it would seem intuitively evident that people, who lack the grammarian's technical terminology, constantly exhibit tacit use of nonterminal categories. This is simply to say, for example, that such people, in judging the grammaticality of unfamiliar, or even meaningless, sentences (or in finding completions for unfinished sentences) constantly exhibit an understanding that certain word combinations are acceptable (or unacceptable) because they present (or do not) a familiar and acceptable combination of grammatical categories. The familiar example—*colorless green ideas sleep furiously*—is recognized as "sounding like English" by someone with no technical grammatical vocabulary simply because it has the same abstract character (makes use of the same nonterminal symbols in its generations) as *colorless old men love furiously, scruffy street cats yowl horribly, filthy rich capitalists shout savagely, mindless red bureaucrats rule rapaciously.* In sense, the actual symbols we have chosen for these abstractions are irrelevant: *Verb, VP, NP,* and so on are also our terminal-symbol *names* for the nonterminal symbols whose purely abstract character derives from the functioning of the grammatical device that we internalize in our capacity to speak and understand English. (Hence, as Chomsky has often observed, the selection and definition of the *vocabulary* of descriptive linguistics, of terms such as *phoneme* and *morpheme* as well as the ones we have mentioned, cannot be carried out without making various presumptions about human psychology.)

The importance of deciding whether a device adequate to the generation of English would make use of nonterminal symbols rests in the light this might cast on the question whether our minds *essentially must* make use of nonterminal abstractions. Much could be said about the proper formulation of this point. But it is clear that a behaviorist view of human psychology would be strengthened if it were established that English could be generated by a grammatical device employing only terminal symbols. Equally, to show that English is not such a language would seem to support mentalism in suggesting that the human mind makes *essential* use of abstractions, that is, of concepts which operate without needing to be named and without appearing to the senses *in any direct way whatsoever*, much less being simple copies of something seen or heard as opposed to essentially internal concepts that function crucially in the mind's acquisition of language.

Much the same general point seems at stake in the question as to whether a finite-state device, pure and simple, is adequate to the generation of the English language. Consider first a finite-state device without loops. Such a device would only produce a finite number of sentences and, simply by the principle that the number of English sentences is not finite, we know that we must finally reject such a grammar. But still, if it were adequate, this would show that (1) someone could know English simply by memorizing all its sentences without needing any knowledge of how they might be generated (or represented more compactly); that is, his knowledge of his language could simply consist of copies of what he had actually heard or seen; and (2) someone could also know English simply in knowing the finite number of states required to generate all its sentences: in other words, the individual would simply learn each state through actual experience, and in this way he would know, given any state, what state could be selected next in constructing sentences. In the first case, one needs no more powerful mental apparatus than memory; in the second, all one requires is a finite number of learned associations of the simplest sort between words. Both possibilities are easily accommodated in the strictest forms of traditional empiricism. Even with loops, which would mean that (1) could not obtain strictly, (2) clearly still remains. All that is added to mental functioning by the loops is the notion that certain kinds of words may be repeated; but one is still operating with the notion of simple associations ("grooved in" by past experience) between copies of past experiences—a notion that was central to traditional empiricism. In David Hume's vocabulary, the words of English would be learned through our senses as "primary impressions" while habituation would provide "secondary impressions" of likely associations between these words.

If English requires a more powerful kind of grammatical device than a finite-state device, then the "software" of the mind must be essentially as powerful as the required device, and this will set a lower limit on the complexity of the actual "hardware." Perhaps, in order to sharpen the discussion, I should now move to the question of how Chomsky *proved* that English is not a finite-state language.

As an aid in explaining Chomsky's proof that English is not a finite-state language, the proof will first be explained for an artificial "letter-word" language and only then for English itself. The proof depends on showing (1) that certain kinds of sentences—"mirror-image" sentences—*can* be generated by a phrase-structure, or rewrite-rule, device; (2) that these kinds of sentences *are* found in some artificial languages and in English; and (3) that these kinds of sentences *cannot* be generated by a finite-state device. Though the proof is not difficult to grasp and Chomsky lays no great emphasis on it in *Syntactic Structures*, I am not alone in thinking that it is one of the most striking pieces of reasoning in Chomsky's early work. Here I will just expand on the argument as it appears in *Syntactic Structures*.

I start by considering two artificial "letter-word" languages, each of which can be generated by two simple phrase-structure, or rewrite, rules. These two kinds of languages appear in the several versions Chomsky has given of the argument. For both languages, II and III, the terminal vocabulary consists of a's and b's, and the nonterminal vocabulary of S's. As usual, the convention is that terminal symbols, which appear in the actual sentences that comprise the language, are lower case, while the nonterminal symbols are capitalized. Language II is generated by the following rules:

(II) (*a*) $S \rightarrow a + b$
    (*b*) $S \rightarrow a + S + b$

[These rules could be written as one rule if parentheses are employed to show that use of the nonterminal symbol is optional—in other words, the rule $S \rightarrow a + (S) + b$ is equivalent to both (IIa) and (IIb).]

Language II is an extremely simple language. It consists of *ab,
aabb, aaabbb, aaaabbbb,* and so on: its sentences include *all
and only* those strings which consist of *n* occurrences of *b* pre-
ceded by *n* occurrences of *a*. After an exposure to a relatively
small number of the sentences of this language, one is likely
to leap to the simplifying assumption that the language as a
whole is generated by rules (IIa) and (IIb). But though this
language can be grasped easily, its sentences cannot be given
by enumeration. Since an *infinite* number of strings are generated
by these rules, this "language" *cannot* be given by listing its
sentences: they *must* be generated by rules; there is no way to
specify the language *except* through the software description
of a generative device.

Though language II is a very simple language and one which
can be generated by two simple rewrite rules, it cannot be generated by a finite-state device. Consider Figure 7.

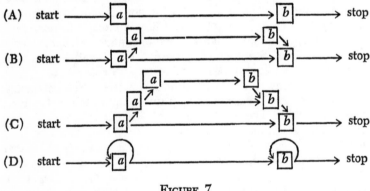

FIGURE 7

The state device (7A), with two boxes, generates one string: *ab.*
Device (7B), with two additional boxes, generates two strings:
ab and *aabb.* Device (7C), with yet two more boxes, generates
three strings: *ab, aabb, aaabbb.* One can proceed in this way as
long as one likes, adding two boxes (that is, two more states)
each time so as to generate one more string. But since the number of strings in the language is infinite, one will never be able
to generate the language by expanding a finite-state device in

this way. One would need an infinite number of boxes, an infinite number of device states, to generate *all and only* those strings that consist of some number of *a*'s followed by exactly the same number of *b*'s.

It is important to write *all and only*. If one reflects on what is generated by device (7D), one sees that (7D) generates *every* string that consists of *any* positive number of *a*'s followed by *any* positive number of *b*'s (for example: *ab, aabb, aaabbb,* and so on, but also *abb, abbb, aab, aaab,* and so on). Device (7D) generates all the sentences of language II. The trouble is that it does not generate *only* the sentences of language II, and hence it is not the grammar of language II. (Similarly, one could generate *all* the sentences of English by means of a finite-state device with one box, containing the words of English, with a recursive loop that would allow one to pick any number of additional words before stopping each string. This device would generate all possible combinations of English words and thus would generate not only all grammatical combinations *but* also all ungrammatical combinations.)

This is an instance of the same limitation in finite-state devices that I have mentioned before. The finite-state device cannot "remember" its previous states—what it can do next is solely determined by the particular state (box) it is in, no matter how many or how few recursive "loopings" the device has undertaken. A device such as (7D) cannot remember how many times *a* has been repeated so that it might then allow exactly the same number of *b* repeats. The only way to ensure an equal number of *a*'s are followed by an equal number of *b*'s with a finite-state device is by adding boxes in the manner of (7A) through (7C) and so on; in this case, it is not that the device remembers its previous states but rather that now the machine is in a *different state* after having produced two *a*'s as opposed to one (or three) *a*'s.

The only way a finite-state device can make sure that some number of *a*'s are followed by the same number of *b*'s is by having as many *a*-boxes as there are *a*'s in the string and as many *b*-boxes as there are *b*'s. Since we are not supposing that there is any particular limit on the length of the sentences of language II, such a language cannot be generated by a device with a finite number of internal states of the sort we have considered. In Figure 7 one finds three finite-state devices that generate *some* of the sentences of language II and no nonsentences, and one finite-state device that generates all the sentences of language II but also countless nonsentences. But no finite-state device can generate all and only the sentences of language II; language II is not a finite-state language.

Next consider language III, generated by rules (IIIa) and (IIIb), which is composed of all strings consisting of any string of *a*'s and *b*'s followed by the mirror-image or reversal of that string (for example, *aa, bb, abba, baab, aaaa, bbbb, abbbba, baaaab*, and so on.)

(III) (a) $S \rightarrow a + (S) + a$
      (b) $S \rightarrow b + (S) + b$

Some thought will suggest that the attempt to generate language through a finite-state device will prove to be impossible, and for essentially the same reason as applied to language *II*.

For example, one might start with two connected *a*-boxes, with a loop from the second back to the first. This will produce *aa, aaaa, aaaaa*, and so on evenly, which is what is wanted. But if one then adds a *b*-box after "start" and then draws a line to the *a*-boxes, one will produce the "ungrammatical" string *baa*; consequently, one will need to add a nonoptional *b*-box after the two *a*'s. After the two beginning *b*'s, one will then need another set of *a*-boxes, followed by two nonoptional *b*-boxes. To sum up: one will need two boxes to get *aa, aaaa, aaaaa*, and so on;; four additional boxes will be needed to get *baab, baaaab, baaaaaab*, and so on; six additional boxes will be needed to get *bbaabb, bbaaaabb, baaaaaab*, and so on. Obviously all such strings could not be generated with a finite-state language.

The next step is to show that English (and, for similar reasons, any natural language) contains similar mirror-image sentences that require for their generation something more powerful than the finite-state devices we have been considering. Broadly, what must be shown is that in many English sentences there are dependencies between words on both sides of an indefinitely expandable intervening phrase (as with language III, one *b* must be followed by one *b*—which thus depends on the prior *b*—no matter how many *a*'s intervene; similarly two *b*'s must be followed by two *b*'s, no matter how many intervening *a*'s; and so on). It is not difficult to show that English has sentences of this sort, that is, sentences which are grammatical in virtue of dependencies between words separated by an indefinite number of phrases having the proper structure. These dependencies cannot be specified except through the use of nonterminal symbols, which means through rules that make essential reference not only to words but to phrase structure above and beyond simple strings of words.

Consider (25), taking *the man who said that* as an *a* and *is arriving today* as a *b*:

(25) The man who said that (S_1) is arriving today

Given that (25) without S_1 is grammatical (that is, *ab*), it is also true that if (25) *replaces* S_1, we still have a grammatical string (*aabb*); and it does not seem wrong to see the process of construction as continuing indefinitely, though the sentences will sound long and a little silly after a time. Thus, *the man who said that—the man who said that is arriving today—is arriving today* is a sentence, and so on. Similarly, *someone who knows that is here* (*ab*) is a sentence; *someone who knows that—someone who knows that is here—is here* (*aabb*) is a sentence; and *someone who knows that—someone who knows that—someone who knows that is here—is here—is here* (*aaabbb*) is also a sentence, and so on. Or, again, *the man knows* (*ab*), *the man the man knows knows* (*aabb*), *the man the man the man knows knows knows* (*aaabbb*), and so on are all sentences. Of course this central embedding of identical sentences is not at all common in English. It is more common to embed nonidentical sentences of similar structure. Sentences, that is, corresponding to *cabd, ecabdf, gecabdfh*, where *ab, cd, ef, gh* are all abstractly of the form $X + Y$ and may be embedded within each other by the rule, $S \rightarrow X + (X + Y) + Y$. In such cases one still finds the dependency (between symbols on either side of an indefinitely expandable phrase structure) that left to right finite-state devices cannot handle.

It is, of course, much much more common in English for such recursive maneuvers to require the deletion, pronominalization

of repeated phrases, and so on. For example, recalling the conjunction problem, if one takes *my father loves old men* (*acb*)
and *my father hates old men* (*aeb*), one can put them together
producing *my father loves and hates old men* only by deleting
repetitions of *my father* (*a*) and *old men* (*b*). The sentence
ac and eb, formed from the underlying *acb and aeb*, has the
sort of dependency that rules out finite-state generation. But
the notion of underlying structure and deletion already presupposes something more powerful than a finite-state machine
and is unnecessarily contentious. Hence, Chomsky chose to
make his case for the inadequacy of finite-state devices through
appeal to the relatively uncommon cases of embedding in which
no deletion is involved.

One can give many more examples of English sentences similar to the mirror-image sentences of language III. In *Syntactic
Structures*, Chomsky uses (25) plus (26) and (27) (with minor
changes in notation):

(26) If S_2, then S_3

(27) Either S_4, or S_5

Chomsky points out the dependencies of the three sentences:
then must always follow *if*, *or* must follow *either*, and *is* must
follow *man*, and these dependencies hold no matter what the
intervening sentence (which may be itself (25), (26), or (27)).
Thus, in (25), taking S_1 to be (26) and S_2 to be (27), we get:

(28) The man who said that if, either S_4 or S_5, then S_3, is
arriving (in effect, *acefdb*)

And so it becomes clear that in English we can have a sequence
of the form $a + S_1 + b$ where *a* and *b* are interdependent; and
we can select in turn as S_1 a sequence of the form $c + S_2 + d$,
with dependency again between *c* and *d*; and then we can pick
a sequence of the form $e + S_3 + f$, with dependency between
e and *f*; and so on. Sequences that violate these dependencies are
not English. Hence, in requiring the construction of mirror-
image sentences, any device adequate to the generation of the
sentences of the English language *cannot* be a left to right

finite-state device without nonterminal symbols. We formulate this as follows:

(G) English is not a finite-state language.

Note that while this argument is a specfic realization of Chomsky's principle that the linguist must show how the infinity of sentences that compose a natural language can be generated through finite means, the argument shows more than that a natural language consists of an infinite number of sentences (E). From (E) it follows that a natural language *cannot* be specified except through specifying a generative device, a device that employs recursion. But from the present argument it also follows that the device must be more powerful than a finite-state device with recursive loops, even though such a device does have the capacity of generating an infinite number of sentences.

I have devoted a great deal more space to this argument than Chomsky did in *Syntactic Structures*. My reason is twofold. First, my experience has been that people who have little or no familiarity with this general sort of argument may fail to grasp the argument in its entirety, to appreciate its force and limits, if the argument is not explained at length and with some repetitions. People have been confused about it even in print. Secondly, the argument already contains, at least in miniature, the most basic elements in Chomsky's approach to language. The basic philosophic and psychological issues, and Chomsky's way of reasoning about theory, are on the table, at least in embryo.

Of course, from the point of view of a practicing linguist particularly interested in some approximation of part of the grammar of English, absolutely nothing of any importance or interest has been said. But as Chomsky's reasoning about the nature of grammar proceeds—in the argument of *Syntactic Structures* that English is a tranformational-generative grammar with particular sorts of rules, in the further developments found in the "standard theory" of *Aspects of the Theory of Syntax*, and in the "extended standard theory" of his most recent papers —the basic principles of this argument are employed again and again, though the applications are much more complicated, and the results of course much closer to an adequate simulation of our grammatical knowledge than this extremely elementary initial step. The argument that an adequate description of a natural language can only be given through specification of a generative device (whose software the competent speaker of the language must minimally internalize) remains constant, though the specification of the requirements that characterize the device has become much more detailed. Equally constant is the claim that natural language sentences have an *abstract* or *deep structure* that *cannot* be explicated by a physical description of such sentences (as noise) and that is not present in a simple sensory, or observational, characterization of such sequences of noise "bounded by silence" (though deep structure has become ever more abstract and complex as the theory has developed, leading in the past few years to a split between transformational-generative linguists on precisely how abstract deep structure must be).

Since the concern of this book is with introducing the more philosophic aspects of Chomsky's work, I feel the needs of the account are best served by emphasizing this initial and basic instance of Chomsky's strikingly original way of reasoning about man's linguistic capacities. Another aspect of this justification is that this particular argument, which is the *first* examination of a grammatical model in *Syntactic Structures*, obviously has psychological and philosophic implications. There is very little to be said for the claim of some linguists that Chomsky's early work was a ground-breaking contribution to linguistic theory that can be easily separated from the "alien and irrelevant" psychological and philosophic "speculations" of his later work.

II *Phrase-Structure Transformational Grammars:* Syntactic Structures

Artificial language II of the last section is perhaps the simplest language one can imagine that must, at minimum, be specified by a phrase-structure, as against a finite-state, grammar. Rule (IIc) [which joins (IIa) and (IIb)], that is, can only generate language II by making use of nonterminal symbols in deriving the sentences of the language by progressively rewriting one symbol (S) as two, or three, symbols.

(II) (c) $S \rightarrow a + (S) + b$

In effect, in deriving particular sentences, the generative device assigns these sentences structural descriptions. Specifically, the derived string of terminal symbols is bracketed into phrase segments. Such a bracketing, as has been mentioned (see Figure 4), is equivalent to a tree diagram. Thus rule (IIc) generates, in deriving the terminal string *aaabbb*, the bracketed structure [*a* [*a* (*ab*) *b*] *b*], and this bracketing is equivalent to a tree (Figure 8) which begins, at the highest or most abstract level, with an S that splits into an *a* plus another S plus a *b*, with the S splitting twice more until all nonterminal symbols are removed in the final level of the tree.

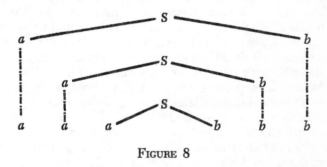

FIGURE 8

Before I present Chomsky's argument that a phrase-structure grammar is not adequate to the generation and structural description of the sentences of English, I might recapitulate the points made in the previous chapter about the connection between structural linguistics and phrase-structure grammars. Chomsky's most basic criticism of structural linguistics is that it did not recognize that since a natural language consists of an infinite number of sentences, it is impossible to list such a body of sentences or to claim that the sentences of such an infinite body may be each simply inferred as more probable than any alternatives from the finite list of sentences that the linguist *has* collected (and described). Hence, as against the most ambitious views of structuralists, the grammarian must be concerned essentially with specifying a generative device. The generative device is not a convenient way of summarizing a (finite) list of sentences—it is the *only* way of adequately describing the phenomena. But Chomsky bolstered this very general criticism by claiming (1) that structural linguists *implicitly* assumed, by their practice in describing sentences, that insofar as a natural language might be described by specifying a set of rules, which would constitute the software of a generative device, the rules would be nothing more powerful than phrase-structure rules; and (2) that such a phrase-structure generative device seemed in no way able to provide a concise and revealing characterization of the sentences of English.

What I should like to do now is to show in a very elementary and incomplete way what features of English lend themselves to phrase structure characterization and what features seem to show that such characterization is insufficient for the full description of English grammar. In particular, I will try to show why a device that can generate, and so structurally describe, the sentences of English needs not only phrase-structure rules but also still more powerful transformational rules.

It has not been possible to offer a clear proof, in the manner of the last section, that a phrase-structure device *cannot* generate the grammatical strings of English (though, ironically, this has been possible with respect to an American Indian language, Mohawk). But it is possible to argue that a transformational grammar may generate the sentences of English in a simpler sort of way and that such a grammar will provide these sentences with more adequate structural descriptions. Because grammars may generate the same strings of terminal symbols (i.e., may agree in *weak* generative capacity), while they may diverge in the structural descriptions that they provide these strings (i.e., may disagree in *strong* generative capacity), one might put the point equally well by saying that Chomsky has shown that phrase-structure grammars fail to have a strong generative capacity that is faithful to the most minimal intuitions of English speakers about the surface structure of English sentences.

The sentence *my father loves men*, for example, can be generated by the simple rules of (20) which is repeated here for convenience.

(20)   (i)   Sentence $\rightarrow$ NP + VP
        (ii)   NP $\rightarrow$ (D) + N

    (iii) VP → Verb + NP
    (iv) D → my, their, the, etc.
    (v) N → father, mother, etc.
    (vi) Verb → loves, hates, etc.

But, as I have tried to show (page 92), when one thinks about expanding these rules to account for the conjunctive sentence *my father loves men and women* (or *my father loves old men and women*), particularly when considering many related conjunctive processes that involve grammatical categories other than nouns, it would be clumsy and unrevealing to account for this by separate rules for conjunction involving verbs, nouns, adverbs, adjectives, etc.

It is possible, however, to account for all such forms of conjunction through one *generalized transformational* rule (again repeated):

(24) $U + Y + W; U + Z + W \rightarrow U + Y + and + Z + W$

    (Where U and W represent identical terminal strings of symbols and Y and Z are identical nonterminal elements that may be realized as different terminal symbols)

Rule (24) is a generalized transformation in that its input consists of two (or more) structures that could be realized as individual sentences. It covers a variety of conjunctive phenomena by constructing any sentence with a conjunction from two structures that could themselves be sentences and consist of the same words except for the Y and Z which, though they are in the same category, may be different words in the sentence that is finally derived by means of the transformation.

Though the details are complicated, the basic idea behind generalized transformations is extremely simple. Aside from some very simple kinds of sentences, such as those generated by (20), one might say that most English sentences—sentences with conjunction for example—*look as if* they could have been constructed by taking two or more very simple sentences and then joining them by means of transformations which delete repetitions of words and phrases in a variety of ways. Instead of using phrase-structure rules to generate simple sentences—or *kernel* sentences, to use Chomsky's term for them—and then adding more and more phrase-structure rules to expand these sentences, Chomsky proposes that a simpler and more revealing grammar will first employ a small number of phrase-structure rules to generate kernel sentences and then employ the more powerful transformational rules to join and rearrange these forms. Rule (24), for example, accounts in one general rule for the generation of (29), (30), (31), and (32) from the simple sentences that accompany them. A number of apparently unrelated phrase-structure rules would be needed to generate these sentences from selected simple sentences, but in that case one would not only have more rules but one would have lost a more revealing and more general rule.

> (29)   My father loves and hates men
>   (*From*: My father loves men, My father hates men)
> (30)   My father loves men and women
>   (*From*: My father loves men, My father loves women)
> (31)   My father and mother love men
>   (*From*: My father loves men, My mother loves men)
> (32)   My father loves and my mother hates men
>   (*From*: My father loves men, My mother hates men)

Once one starts, one sees that generality and simplicity can be got in a great variety of ways by applying a relatively small number of generalized transformations to the kernel strings produced by ten or so phrase-structure rules. One will, for example, need to have phrase-structure rules to generate structures of the form *Noun + Verb + Adjective* in such a way that grammaticality is maintained (*Nancy is old*, not *Nancy are old*, and so on). Simplicity and generality are served if one has a nominalizing transformation that will convert this structure into *Adjective + Noun* (*old Nancy*) while joining it with another structure to make a complete sentence. Sentence (33), which is generated by the tangle of boxes in the state diagram of Figure 6, will be generated in a transformational-generative grammar by nominalizing transformations acting on (34) and (35) to embed them in (36) [with (37) representing something like an intermediate stage on the way to the highly contracted (33)].

(33) Invisible God created the visible world
(34) God is invisible (*Becomes*: invisible God)
(35) The world is visible (*Becomes*: the visible world)
(36) God created the world
(37) God who is invisible created the world which is visible

Chomsky found (33) (or rather its French equivalent, *Dieu invisible a créé le monde visible*) in the Port-Royal *Grammar* (1660), a product of a number of rationalist linguist-logicians whose work derived in good measure from the rationalist philosophy propounded by René Descartes. Chomsky was happy to find that his transformational-generative machinery provided a way of solidifying and further justifying their claim that (37)—composed of the three separate propositions (34), (35), and (36)—underlies the surface form (33).

But it is a *singulary transformation* (one that operates on a *single* phrase-structure product, not two or more) that is possibly the most familiar instance of the revealing and economic character of transformational rules. Consider the relationship between (38) and its passive counterpart (39):

(38) Jack hit John
(39) John was hit by Jack

A phrase-structure grammar would need one set of rules to generate (38) and similar forms. But one singulary transformation (40) can take the place of all these additional rules because *if* the active form, which is the input for the transformation, is grammatical, *then* the passive output will also be grammatical, without the need for additional rules.

(40) $NP_1 + Verb + NP_2 \rightarrow NP_2 + was + Verb + by + NP_1$
(This is a simplified version of the actual rule)

It is almost impossible not to believe that there is a very close syntactical relationship between (38) and (39)—just the sort of relationship that is expressed by rule (40). A sense of this relationship seems to be part of the intuitions of an ordinary speaker of English in just the way that the phrase-structure segmentation of *my father loves old men and women* into *my father—loves—old men and women* seems to be part of his intuitions. But there is no way that this relationship can be given clear or adequate expression in a phrase-structure grammar. The singulary transformation (40) shows us how (38) gives rise to (39) by a formal reshuffling of elements. But there is simply no way of getting from (38) to (39) by means of a phrase-structure tree. A phrase-structure grammar rewrites single, nonterminal symbols until none are left; but (40) has three symbols as input, none of which is rewritten as something else, rather being shuffled about, and the subscript numbers "look ahead" to the actual terminal symbols because they require that the same words appear as input subject and output object (NP_1) and as input object and output subject (NP_2).

In *Syntactic Structures* Chomsky wished to emphasize the purely formal character of syntax and our intuitive knowledge of it as ordinary speakers. This formal syntax could be described without bringing in the then nebulous topic of linguistic meaning. Hence there was no provision for a *semantic component*, in addition to syntax and phonology, in the grammar of *Syntactic Structures*. Indeed, Chomsky stressed (pages 100–101) that the purely syntactical relationship between active and passive that is expressed by a rule like (40) *is not to be explained as a result of equivalence in meaning* because some passive transforms are not equivalent in meaning to their active counterparts. In particular, he pointed out that a *quantificational sentence* such as *everyone in this room knows at least two languages* is not equivalent in meaning to its passive transform *at least two languages are known by everyone in this room*. Why? Because what the active form means would be true even if each person in the room has no language in common, while the passive form strongly suggests that two particular languages are known by everyone in the room.

I will return to this example, and the issue of whether transformations such as passive change meaning, later in the chapter. The subject is interesting because in *Aspects of the Theory of Syntax* Chomsky adopted the principle, which was championed by J. J. Katz and P. M. Postal, that transformations should never be written in such a way as to change meaning. In

Aspects, a semantic component is added to grammar, with *pre-transformational* syntactical structures providing the input to the semantic component and *posttransformational* structures providing the input to the phonological component; the assumption that transformations do not change meaning helps make this system elegant and coherent, as we will see in the next section.

In *Syntactic Structures*, the passive transformation is considered *optional*. This means that the input structure does not have to undergo the transformation, that is, it will become a grammatical sentence without this step as is the case, of course, with the active counterparts of the passive transforms. There are some *obligatory* transformations in the grammar of *Syntactic Structures*—for example the transformation that helps ensure that the subject noun and the verb will agree in having plural or singular forms—but though the four that Chomsky specifies there cover some apparently complex and chaotic grammatical matters in an ingenious and strikingly simple way, I will not say anything more about them.

Aside from the passive, there are five other optional transformations clearly specified in *Syntactic Structures*. In company with the passive, such transformations will produce all the sentences of (41) from one abstract underlying string, which most closely resembles (41i) because that sentence is derived without any optional transformations.

(41) (i)   Harry loves the army
        (ii) The army is loved by Harry
        (iii) Does Harry love the army
        (iv) What does Harry love
        (v)   Who loves the army
        (vi) Harry doesn't love the army
              (And so on)

It is quite easy to see the strength of Chomsky's argument that transformational grammars are simpler and more revealing than purely phrase-structure grammars. And those linguists who have followed Chomsky's lead in trying to write grammars that are general, explicit, and formal have not made a serious effort to write phrase-structure grammars for natural language; such grammars simply are not in the running any longer. But serious theoretical questions continue to be raised about *simplicity* and *revealing-ness*. Precisely how simplicity is to be measured is a difficult question both when one is talking about a sense of simplicity that is peculiar to human languages (and human language acquisition) and when one is talking about the general sense of simplicity that is an important factor in all scientific theories, whether concerned with language or any other phenomena. While the case for the greater simplicity of transformational grammars would seem overwhelming on any measure, Chomsky has insisted that the crucial notion of simplicity for linguistic theory is one that will ultimately derive from the theory of language acquisition. Though there is a notion of absolute, or general, simplicity, which applies to theories in physics as much as to theories in psychology, this notion is not a crucial one for linguistic theory, however absorbing its study is for the philosophy of science. In other words, Chomsky thinks grammars should reflect what is simple for us, what we find easy to learn and employ, thus meeting the goal of explanatory adequacy. If two grammars generate the same sentences and structural descriptions, thus meeting the requirements of observational and descriptive adequacy in the same way, then to say that one is linguistically simpler than the other is to say that it is simpler, or more easily learned, than the other for human beings.

The problem of measuring how revealing grammars are is more practical and psychological. Most linguists would agree that the ordinary speaker of English does have an intuitive sense of the structure of English sentences, that is, a rough sense of sentences splitting into phrases and some equally rough sense of transformational relationships between sentences. But one cannot place too much weight on these intuitions. In the early years of transformational-generative linguistics, many people, including perhaps Chomsky himself, felt that it would be possible within a few years to produce a grammar of English that would be observationally and descriptively adequate, deriving from a body of sentences and structural descriptions that nearly any ordinary fluent speaker of English would find acceptable. It was thought that borderline cases, where ordinary speakers would not agree on whether a sentence or structural description was acceptable, would not be of crucial importance or interest; the grammar itself, which would be based on the much larger body of clear cases, might decide these doubtful cases. However, in recent years many transformational-generative grammarians have based arguments about parts of the grammar of English, and other natural languages, on very subtle and doubtful evidence about what ordinary speakers are supposed to find acceptable, or unacceptable, in the way of sentences or structural properties of sentences.

A few linguists have waved aside such evidential worries by stating that they mean to talk, not about English, but about their own personal version of English—"my idiolect" as they sometimes put it. The potential indistinguishability of data and theory that this practice suggests reminds me, at least, of the habit of some Freudian psychologists, including Freud himself, of making claims about processes in the human mind simply on the basis of extremely subtle evidence in the mental experience of the psychologist himself. The transformational-generative linguists who are in principle most prone to this practice, often called "generative semanticists," do not command the full sympathy of Chomsky, whose current position is that of the "interpretive semanticists," to use the common jargon.

Some psychological experiments with adults and children, while roughly confirming many of Chomsky's basic claims, have also shown that it is easy to exaggerate the uniformity and depth of ordinary speakers' intuitions about language. But certainly one might say that a portion of these problems are natural to the development of a new theory and methodology. After an initial period during which many scientists assimilate a radically new theoretical viewpoint, it is wholly natural for them to begin to fix their attention on more difficult, ambitious, and subtle problems and to become more aware of limitations in the new program. The general battle for acceptance of the new viewpoint has been won, and internal division and criticism begin. Both the specific linguistic problem of simplicity and that of the characterization of ordinary speakers' intuitions about structure (revealing-ness) are basic to the Chomskyan program of progressively narrowing the characterization of our linguistic software, both to describe the mind more specifically and to gain some notion of the brain's hardware through this characterization.

Perhaps I might finish this account of the argument for transformational grammars by discussing a phrase whose analysis has captured the imagination of those concerned with language more than any other mentioned in *Syntactic Structures*. Consider the question of whether there is any ambiguity in (42i):

(42)   (i)   The shooting of the hunters awakened me
        (ii)   The hunting of the lions was bloody
        (iii) The painting of the artist is now at an end

Many individuals interpret (42i) to mean: *the hunters shot* (their guns)—*this awakened me*. But there is another way to hear the sentence: *someone shot the hunters—this awakened me.* Two points about this ambiguity are crucial to Chomsky's argument: (1) it is *structural*, having to do with syntactical construction; and (2) it cannot be accounted for in terms of phrase structure-bracketing.

One way to see that the ambiguity of (42i) is structural is to note that the same ambiguity is present in (42ii) and (42iii). In none of these three cases does the ambiguity depend on the fact that one particular word (in one of the constructions or in any other) has two meanings. If I say, "Meet me at the bank," what I say is ambiguous *semantically* because the word "bank" has two dictionary meanings: *financial institution* or *solid boundary of a body of water*. But what I say has the same syntactical generation, the same grammatical structure, whichever I happen to have in mind when I say "bank."

As I have pointed out, the structural ambiguity of *old men and women* can be represented by bracketing in derivations generated by phrase-structure grammar (though, of course, the same effect could be obtained by just one generalized transformation operation on different underlying kernels). The phrase is bracketed so that it either reads *old* (*men and women*) or (*old men*) and (*women*). But a moment's reflection reveals that no simple phrase-structure bracketing is going to explain the ambiguity of structure in (42). There is no way to put the parentheses that will suggest the relevant ambiguity.

In the transformational grammar of *Syntactic Structures* a phrase of the form *the* $+ V + ing + of + NP_1$ [as in (42)] can be derived transformationally from either of two kernels: either from $NP_1 + V$ (*the hunters shoot*) or from $NP_2 + V + NP_1$ (*they shoot the hunters*). In the first case "the hunters" is, logically and transformationally, the subject of the sentence; in the second case, it is the object. Similarly, (42ii) could derive from *the lions hunt*..., with "lions" as object. And (42iii) could derive from *the artist paints*... or ... *paints the artist*.

On the other hand, sentences (43i) and (43ii), while they appear identical in structure to those of (42) in terms of surface bracketing, are not ambiguous.

(43)   (i)   The screaming of the gulls awakened me
       (ii) The bombing of the building awakened me

Within a transformational grammar there is a simple explanation of our intuition (our untutored perception) that (43i) and (43ii) are not ambiguous. The explanation is that neither (43i) nor (43ii) has two underlying kernels, one where the noun of the surface subject phrase is subject, the other where it is object, with the one ambiguous sentence deriving from either kernel by different transformations. In particular, sentence (43i) derives from the underlying kernel *the gulls scream* in which the noun of the surface subject phrase, *gulls*, is the deep subject. But *they scream the gulls* is not a possible kernel (because the phrase-structure rules would not provide the basis for its generation); hence there is no input for the transformation which would carry an underlying string into sentence (43i) in which the underlying object, *the gulls*, becomes part of the surface subject. For much the same reason there is no ambiguity in (43ii). Sentence (43ii) derives from *they* (or whatever) *bomb the building*, in which *the building* is the grammatical object. But there is no ambiguity because a kernel in which *the building* is the subject—namely, *the building bombs*...— is not possible. It is difficult to see any way of explaining why the sentences of (42), but not those of (43), are ambiguous without assuming a system of tranformations operating on underlying strings.

A similar well-known example, which Chomsky and others have used, is sentence (44):

(44)   Flying planes can be dangerous

This sentence is structurally ambiguous—either suggesting that those who fly planes can be so endangered, or that planes, which fly about, can be dangerous—and transformational grammar accounts for this ambiguity in showing that two rather different underlying strings could be transformed into the same sentence. Of course, there is absolutely no suggestion that the ordinary competent speaker of English is *conscious* of such transformations—either the transformations of *Syntactic Structures* or those that might appear in the more precise grammars of future research—when he speaks, or hears, such a sentence; what he is conscious of, or can easily be brought to see, is simply that such sentences are ambiguous, and this fact must appear in the structural descriptions provided English sentences in an adequate grammar.

What these examples purport to show is that if one assumes (F1)—briefly, that an adequate grammatical characterization of a language must amount to the specification of a device which will generate (weak capacity) the sentences of the language and assign (strong capacity) them proper structural descriptions—one should conclude that

(H)   English is not a phrase-structure language.

The argument may be summarized as follows: (1) the ordinary speaker of English recognizes that (42i), (42ii), (42iii), and (44) are structurally ambiguous, while (43i) and (43ii) are not structurally ambiguous; (2) hence a descriptively adequate English grammar should generate (strong capacity) structural descriptions that show this ambiguity and lack of ambiguity; and (3) a phrase-structure grammar cannot generate structural descriptions that show this (certainly it cannot do so in any simple or natural way, that is, by familiar forms of bracketing, and so on). Our knowledge of the structure of such sentences is of a highly abstract, or mentalistic, character and is in no way equivalent to the straightforward segmentation of explicit surface strings that structural linguists seem to have had in mind. Not only are nonterminal symbols required in the generation of English, but we also require underlying nonterminal strings, or deep structures, as they have come to be called. Considering the enormous generative power that transformations add to grammatical devices, one presumably need not look for some essentially more powerful form of generative device. Hence:

(I) English is a transformational language. (Similar analyses have been produced for a very substantial number of other natural languages, so one might speculate that "A human language" could replace "English.")

Before I give a general summary of the grammar of *Syntactic Structures*, I will briefly remind the reader of the point, which I made in the Introduction, that one could say that a crucial factor in the Chomskyan revolution has been the introduction and justification of more powerful modes of description that make the older (structuralist) modes of description appear—startlingly—as a "special case" of this more powerful mode. In the Introduction I suggested, as a rather extravagant analogy, that one could compare this to Einstein's discovery that all that seemed possible in a Newtonian physical universe appears as a special Euclidean case within the more powerful descriptive system that Einstein made available through use of non-Euclidean geometry. The argument against the phrase-structure grammar of structural linguistics is one that shows that such a mode of description is a special case—though roughly sufficient to a good portion of familiar linguistic phenomena—within the much more powerful characterizations that transformational grammar can provide. For that matter, the argument that phrase-structure grammars are more adequate than finite-state devices has the same form, as does that against the still less powerful level of descriptive capacity provided by nonrecursive, or loopless, finite-state devices (or by that provided by simple enumeration of sentences).

In summary, the grammar sketched in *Syntactic Structures* consists of three sorts of rules, which operate in sequence in generating the sentences of English and in providing them with phonological realizations in speech.

1. Phrase-structure rules which rewrite single, nonterminal symbols into, eventually, terminal symbols or words, in this manner creating a tree diagram or phrase-structure bracketing.

2. Transformational rules, which operate upon the phrase

structures produced by (1), deleting, reshuffling, and joining portions of such structures. (Singulary transformations, whose input is single phrase-structure (kernel) strings, are either obligatory or optional, optional transformations including passive, negative, and question transformations. Generalized transformations, which are always optional, join two or more kernel strings. As opposed to the phrase-structure rules, transformations are ordered, in that some must be applied after others—the passive transformation, for example, must apply *before* the transformation that makes the verb plural or singular, and so on, because it is the noun that is put into subject position by the passive transformation that determines the form of the verb.

3. Morphophonemic rules, which convert the output of (2), the sentences of the language from a syntactical viewpoint, into the actual sounds of speech. (These rules, of which no account has been given here, are similar to the phrase-structure rules. But they allow the rewriting of *more* than one symbol, and they are "context-sensitive" in that they may indicate that a symbol is to be rewritten in a particular way *only if* certain symbols precede or follow that symbol. For example, the purely syntactical rules (1) and (2) will generate strings such as *take + past-tense*; the rule that will convert that segment into the sounds that we write as "took" is a morphophonemic rule.)

If one has grasped the nature of these rules, and the general structure of the grammar that is summarized here, one will not find it difficult to follow the changes that are brought in with the "standard theory" of *Aspects of the Theory of Syntax* (1965), and in still more recent work. I mention this because the reader may feel that he has been burdened with enough of a technical apparatus, and so he has. Perhaps the major change that takes place is that *meaning* becomes a respectable and central part of linguistics: to the *syntactical* and *phonological* components that may be found in the first version of the theory, *Aspects* adds a third *semantic* component. The formulation of this component, and its relationship to the others, will be seen as a major theater of controversy. The phonological component undergoes radical changes in *The Sound Pattern of English* (1968), which Chomsky coauthored with his MIT colleague Morris Halle. In that book considerable evidence is marshaled for the view that the input from the syntactical component is manipulated by a cycle of phonological rules that have the same power as the transformational rules of syntax.

III *The Grammar of* Aspects of the Theory of Syntax *and Some More Recent Developments*

Until the publication of *Syntactic Structures* (1957) and the appearance of his work in conferences on linguistic analysis at the University of Texas (1958, 1959), Chomsky's work was not generally available, or availing, among linguists. Indeed, the better portion of his earliest work appeared more in publications devoted to mathematical, logical, philosophic, or psychological topics than in publications aimed primarily at professional linguists. His bulky manuscript, "The Logical Principles of Linguistic Theory" (1955), from which *Syntactic Structures* was excerpted, is the more amazing in sweep and complexity in that it represents the largely solitary creation of a wholly new way of doing linguistics, and of new areas in linguistic research. Though Chomsky caused some ripples in the local intellectual community while putting together the manuscript with the support of a Junior Fellowship at Harvard University (1951–55), it is now a familiar story that MIT Press declined to publish the manuscript and that the Dutch publisher Mouton published *Syntactic Structures* because one of their representatives happened to be curious about the excerpted version of the manuscript that Chomsky used for his classes at MIT.

During the late 1950's and early 1960's, however, Chomsky had gathered round him a large, excited, and brilliant group of linguists, psychologists, and philosophers, some starting their professional work under the new aegis, others with functioning careers, often converts from structural linguistics, behavioristic psychology, or related radically empiricist views. It would be fascinating to write (or read) the history of the manner in which this "new science" spread among people of the university and research institutions of the Cambridge, Massachusetts, and Boston intellectual community. It spread through mimeographed articles—because print was too slow a process—and through seminars and "personal communication" when even the mimeo-

graph machine meant too long a wait (a typical journal article
in Chomskyan linguistics will contain a bibliography with perhaps more than half its entries referring to mimeographed items,
and, indeed, many papers will have had their influence, been
criticized, defended, and become out of date, all before their
actual appearance in print). This would also be a history of
the geographic spread of the new science as the intellectual
communities of Berkeley, Chicago, and New York were seeded
with Chomskyan Ph.D.'s or spontaneously converted; equally,
it would be a passionate and acrimonious history, with all the
extremes of patricidal and fratricidal emotions that are inevitably
present in genuinely serious, large scale, intellectual and scientific
debates. Intriguing and naughty as it would be to put together
such a history, I shall practice restraint here.

Not only am I going to ignore these matters of the social
history of the spread of a new paradigm of scientific research,
but I will also hardly attempt to give any sort of an account
of the various individual contributions made in the many papers
that followed on the heels of *Syntactic Structures* and that led
to the construction and formulation of the "standard theory"
that is authoritatively summarized and examined in *Aspects of
the Theory of Syntax*. Rather, I will briefly summarize the most
significant change in the theory—the development of a semantic
component, of the inclusion, that is, of a theory of meaning as
part of the task of constructing grammars for natural languages.
This summary will consist of three parts: (1) the nature of
the changes in the layout of a natural language grammar; (2)
the reasons provided for these changes *that have a purely syntactical basis*; and (3) the reasons for these changes, happily
seconding the syntactical reasons, that relate to semantic, psychological, philosophic, and logical considerations. I will round
this section off by briefly explaining the interpretive semanticist-
generative semanticist controversy which has, in some not alto-
gether fundamental ways, split the ranks of transformational-
generative grammarians. I will end the whole chapter with one
criticism that is commonly offered against transformational-generative grammarians, and with at least some reply to this
criticism.

One reason I will be so brief on developments subsequent to

Syntactic Structures is that Chomsky's most significant general
views about linguistics, and his views about psychology and
philosophy, are explicitly stated or implied in that first work.
Another reason is that it is sometimes wrongly implied—as I
have mentioned—that his mentalistic and antibehaviorist views
about psychology, and his resurrection of philosophical rationalism, stem from a supposedly unfortunate and wildly speculative
extrapolation, through questionable analogies, of his original
work; my method of exposition should indicate both that this
interpretation is misplaced and that there has been a genuine
continuity in Chomsky's thought. A final reason—and here I
interject my personal and contentious view—is that the motivat-
ing thrust in the developments that led to the standard theory,
and beyond to generative semantics, is an attempt to provide
a "semantics of natural language" or a "natural logic" which will,
among other things, enable the professional linguist to provide,
as professional service, authoritative answers to most of the
problems that have concerned analytic philosophers and philosophical logicians in this century. And I think this thrust has
been in good measure mistaken, that the recent split within
transformational-generative grammar has shown the nature of
the difficulty, and that this mode of exposition will give the
best sort of short picture of the issues.

The story of the major change can best be told by reiterating
what it is a change from. In *Syntactic Structures,* Chomsky
emphasized the *independence* of grammaticality, of linguistic
well-formedness, from meaning or meaningfulness, with good
reason. What was being stressed was, in effect, the independence—
the purely formal, syntactical, and narrowly linguistic character—of grammaticality and of the characterization of the
generative device (the minimal psychological software) that is
essentially knit with the specification of grammaticality. Chomsky
accepted the view that an adequate grammar should specify a
language by generating, and providing structural descriptions
for, the sentences of the language. Since natural languages do
not consist of finite numbers of sentences, they can only be
described by specification of the software of a generative device.
Given the recursive and abstract character of English, and other
natural languages, the minimal software must be a (phrase

structure plus) transformational device, with both nonterminal symbols and nonterminal structures.

Since we have the same generative capacities (at least) of such a device—as is simply revealed in our ability to play Sentence Scrabble® and implicitly in our more complicated everyday linguistic activity—we have the software capacities in question too: we are, among other things, transformational devices that make use of nonterminal symbols and structures (of mentalistic abstractions). Further, the linguist, with a finite corpus from which to derive the grammar of a language, has no determinate way of arriving at the right grammar—at least not without a general explanatory theory of human language and of language acquisition (in that the child, faced with a much more inadequate sample, does come up with an adequate notion of the grammar of the sampled language). And so it follows that an adequate grammatical, or linguistic, character-ization of a language is presumably going to involve, eventually, some notion of the software of language acquisition and hence some notion of features universal to human languages. From all this one can derive, as I have sketched, a certain support for mentalism and innateness in psychology, and for the philosophic rationalism that Chomsky has come to champion; equally the opposition to behaviorism and radical empiricism is apparent from Chomsky's first discussion of a generative device.

But it is notable that Chomsky made it clear that this specifica-tion of syntactic structure takes place without any dependence on the notion of meaning, i.e., on a possible semantic component to grammars. In succeeding paragraphs, I will mention some specific replies that Chomsky gave in *Syntactic Structures* to arguments that purported to show that syntax must be based on semantics.

But first I should mention two very general background considerations which had, with little doubt, some force. First, Chomsky started by accepting the problem of describing a language as a structuralist would see it (though he recon-structed the structuralist's position in generative terms), and this led him to the specification of a device that would generate, and provide structural descriptions for, the sentences of the language. Chomsky tried to show that the generative device would have to have transformational power, which clearly meant that the agreed goal could not be attained by structuralist means and thus meant that structuralism was inadequate. This line of criticism depended on accepting the (reconstructed) structuralist viewpoint about the goal of a grammatical description of a language. Secondly, if not for structuralist reasons alone, Chomsky felt sympathy for this formal view of what constitutes a grammar. He shared with the structuralists the view that (1) meaning did not lend itself to specification within the formal means that ought to, or even could, be provided for in grammar proper; and (2) that problems of meaning—determining whether sentences were meaningful or "make sense," whether sentences had the same or different meanings, and what sentences actually mean, their reference and truth conditions—would involve linguists in questions that belonged as much, or more, to logic and to the conceptual and empirical problems of various sciences. At the time, Chomsky took the view (of Nelson Goodman) that meaning was a matter of the reference of words and the utterances in which they served. Obviously a formal system is not going to specify (that is, literally point out) what the various things are that words stand for, or the various situations that satisfy the propositions we put forward.

Chomsky, of course, has since discarded this Goodmanian radical empiricist view of meaning. But Chomsky has retained the view that syntax can, and should be, developed *autonomously*, independently of meaning, and that insofar as the linguist has the subsequent and dependent task of specifying a semantic component, this mandate, at least for the foreseeable future, does not put the linguist in any authoritative position so far as the problems people in other disciplines have concerning the meaning of various terms, that is, concerning the logical properties of theoretical propositions formulated in natural language.

For example, Chomsky often stresses that the structuralists were not in a position to define "utterance," "phoneme," "morpheme," "sentence," "constituent," "human language," and so on, in whatever way they wished; rather, these theoretical terms carry in their definitions various general, empirical presuppositions about man and his languages, and any "method in structural linguistics" that defines these terms makes basic claims about

the logical subject. It is precisely this line of thought that led to the grammar of *Aspects*.

Thirdly, Chomsky considered the claim that an active sentence and its corresponding passive are synonymous (in effect, the claim that the passive transformation preserves meaning). As mentioned above (page 100), Chomsky points out that quantificational sentences do not preserve meaning under the passive transformation; *everyone in this room knows at least two languages* can be true when its passive transform is false, which is a most dramatic failure to preserve meaning. While the passive transformation characteristically does preserve meaning, it does not in many quantificational sentences and possibly in some other cases (I interject that the reason for calling sentences "quantificational" is that they contain words such as "everyone," "someone," and so on, which function in the same way as the universal and existential quantifiers of predicate logic). Chomsky stresses (p. 101) that *the important point about transformations is that they preserve grammaticality*. With many of the transformations (aside from the passive itself) such as the negative and interrogative, it is absolutely clear that meaning is changed by the transformation.

It is a clue to the developments that led to *Aspects* and beyond that while a sentence and its corresponding negative transform preserve grammaticality and obviously do not preserve sameness of meaning, the change in meaning from the sentence to its negative transform is regular, not haphazard, and regular suggests according to rule. What is according to rule presumably can be formalized. Why not add such rules to the description of a language in some way?

In *Syntactic Structures*, Chomsky insists that while there obviously are correspondences between the structures and elements of formal, grammatical analysis and the semantic features and functions of language, these correspondences are "imperfect," "vague," or "inexact"; while they belong to the study of language in a broader sense, "important insights and generalizations" about the formal character of syntactical operations will be lost if grammar (syntax) is asked to account for synonymy, meaningfulness, reference, and, generally, logical relationships between sentences.

To clarify further these points about transformations and meaning, I might say something about the word "transformation." Some time before Chomsky formulated his theories, logicians made use of the terms *formation rule* and *transformation rule*; and their use of the terms, with which Chomsky was familiar, is suggestive. Logicians work with artificial languages, mostly of a simple and abstract character, which have interesting logical features. In specifying such a language, familiarly, the logician will begin by specifying what are sentences, that is, by providing syntactical rules; but he calls the sentences *well-formed formulas*, and the rules that generate them, *formation rules*. These formation rules have the power of phrase-structure (rewrite) rules (though they are often given in a more compact form). Logicians' transformation rules do not, however, have much to do with simulating or extending well-formedness; rather, they preserve truth and, in that sense, meaning. They are the rules of valid argument, which transform premises into conclusions in such a way that whatever conditions will make the premises true, will also make the conclusions true.

Speaking roughly, then, it is fair to say that logicians' transformations preserve meaning (or truth). Within this terminological context it would seem quite clear that Chomsky meant to lay great stress on the generalization that the syntactical transformations of natural language preserve grammaticality (well-formedness) but do not preserve meaningfulness or truth, nor will the specific meaning, or associated truth conditions, of the input necessarily be found in the transformational output. The attempt to base grammar on meaning, to require that grammatical transformations preserve meaning, will lead to the loss of "important insights and generalizations" about purely formal linguistic software.

In the face of this defense of the autonomy of syntax, one still can see respects in which a transformational grammar of the sort *Syntactic Structures* proposes reveals something about meaning. For example, the pretransformational sources of *the shooting of the hunters* do reveal more about meaning than is evident in the posttransformational output (facts such as these lead to the practice in *Aspects* of calling pretransformational input sources deep structures, and the posttransformational outputs surface structures). Though the deep structure in question is justified by purely syntactical arguments, it also happens to account for features of meaning. Again, the change from active to passive usually means that what we might call the logical (or semantic) subject is displaced into object position. What is in subject position in deep structure seems to accord better with the semantic notion of subject. So, once more, though the deep structure in question is justified by purely syntactical arguments, it also happens to account for features of meaning. Again, purely syntactical considerations of generative simplicity seem to justify the notion that (33) *Invisible God created the visible world* is transformationally derived from three separate strings, which as one deep structure would most resemble *God—God is invisible—created the world—the world is visible*, or, after pronominalization, (37) *God, who is invisible, created the world, which is visible*. These deep-structure sources seem to reveal more about the meaning or logical structure than is evident in the surface structure (33). So, once more, though deep structures are justified by purely syntactical arguments, they also happen to account for features of meaning, and do so more fully than surface structures.

Hence the simple thought: if one wants to account for meaning, if one wants to add a semantic component to the characterization of a language, would not the *input* to this semantic component obviously have to be the deep structure of sentences and not surface structure? Hence, also, the inevitable pressure to formulate the structure of the syntactical component so that this deep-structure input will be as apt as possible for its role.

Briefly, one may summarize the three components of the grammar of *Aspects* as follows:

1. A syntactical component, consisting of base rules and transformational rules. The *base* consists of phrase-structure rules as in *Syntactic Structures,* but those rules that rewrite nonterminal symbols as words are dropped in favor of lexical insertion rules, which allow insertion of words from a *lexicon* in accordance with a series of syntactical features (these lexical-insertion rules, which restrict the selection of word combinations, are what function to exclude *colorless green ideas sleep furiously* in the syntax of *Aspects*). The lexicon has the general job of indicating

all and only the phonological, syntactical, or semantic features of particular words that are not predictable from the general rules of phonology, syntax, or semantics. The transformational rules are similar to those of *Syntactical Structures*.

However, in *Aspects* the phrase-structure rules are recursive (that is, the rule *NP* → *Sentence* is added), allowing the production of whole structures like (37), rather than simply generating simple kernels which the transformational rules optionally combine. The deep structure, produced by these recursive phrase-structure rules, is keyed to the application of various transformations, all of which are obligatory. The net effect of these changes is to ensure that each unambiguous surface sentence will have a single deep structure, which will not differ in meaning in any obvious way from the surface structure except in being more revealing and explicit in determining meaning; hence, the deep structure will be the obvious candidate for the input to the semantic component, which presumably will attempt a formal account of meaningfulness and sameness and difference of meaning or, in general, an account of the logical relationships between sentences.

2. A semantic component, consisting of *dictionary entries* (presumably from the lexicon, a compendium of what is peculiar to particular words and must be learned individually) and *projection rules*, so that the syntactical input structures may be assigned a semantic analysis in a formal way. For example, *meet me at the bank* has no syntactical ambiguity, but the dictionary entry for *bank* would mean that the projection rules would assign the sentence two semantic interpretations; hence it is semantically ambiguous. One is invited to assume that this component will simulate, in interpreting the deep structures generated by the base, the competent speaker's intuitions about ambiguity and the logical relations between sentences. The initial work on the structure of this component was largely done by the philosophers J. J. Katz and J. A. Fodor, but their work has been criticized, and there is presently considerable uncertainty about how the component should be put together. Chomsky himself has written little on the structure of the semantic component.

3. A phonological component, consisting of rules through which the surface structures of syntax are rendered into speech sounds.

In *Aspects* these rules can still be regarded as rewrite morphophonemic rules, but since that time Chomsky has explicitly
proposed that a cycle of transformational rules will account much
better for the conversion of surface syntax to sound. Indeed,
Chomsky and Halle have argued for some time that the notion
of the phoneme is suspect, and they propose that the output
of the phonological component should not be strings of phonemes
(belonging to the arbitrary and peculiar "phonemic alphabet" of
the particular language in question) but rather a matrix of dis-
tinctive features that are *universal* to human speech.

As Chomsky writes at the beginning of the 1968 paper, "Deep
Structure, Surface Structure, and Semantic Interpretation":

A grammar of a language, in the sense in which I will use this
term, can be loosely described as a system of rules that expresses
the correspondence between sound and meaning in this language.
Let us assume given two universal language independent systems of
representation, a phonetic system for the specification of sound and
a semantic system for the specification of meaning. As to the former,
there are many concrete proposals. In the domain of semantics there
are, needless to say, problems of fact and principle that have barely
been approached, and there is no reasonably concrete or well-defined
"theory of semantic representation" to which one can refer.

The structure of these proposals of the standard theory of
Aspects and Chomsky's subsequent work is diagrammed in
Figure 9 (p. 121):

One notable point about this figure is that it makes clear a
strong drive to find the universal in language, to provide
representations that are not dependent on particular languages.
A characterization of a language, in Chomsky's firm present
position, should specify in (perhaps quite complicated) formal
terms the correspondences that hold in that language between
sound, represented in a universal way not dependent on the
particular language, and meaning, also so represented. Given
that the rules and components relating these two language-
independent systems are themselves specified in a general, formal,
and explicit way, descriptions of several human languages should
gradually make apparent which rules and linguistic features
are universal to human languages and which are peculiar to
particular languages.

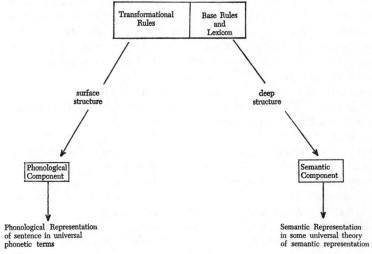

FIGURE 9

Chomsky frequently distinguishes *formal* and *substantive* universals of grammar. Formal universals would have to do with the structure of grammars, of the software that the fluent speaker internalizes. For example, the split into base plus transformational subcomponents, assuming it to be universal to human languages, would be a formal universal. A substantive universal might be the abstract syntactic features *NP* and *VP*: perhaps these might be shown to be universal to human languages. A third sort of grammatical universal that has come to seem particularly important in the years since *Aspects* has negative character: if particular sorts of rules, sorts of transformational manipulations, are never found in human languages, one has *universal constraints* on the form of grammatical rules. For example, some claim that there is a universal constraint against moving material in or out of a conjunctive structure. In English, one cannot pluck *old men* out of the conjunction *old men and women,* so as to derive **old men are loved by my father and women* or **they are loved by my father and women* from *my father loves old men and women* by transformations which are acceptable if they move the *whole* conjunction. If this were generally true, then the *constraint* would be universal. Universal constraints have seemed particularly important to transformational grammarians because, as Chomsky has often emphasized, transformational rules are so powerful that unless such constraints are established there will be by far too many ways of writing the grammars of particular languages. It has been established that, given a few powerful and unnatural transformational rules, one can write a perhaps highly unnatural, but nonetheless observationally adequate, grammar for any possible human language. The existence for universal constraints would be one of the most powerful ways of eliminating such excesses and reducing the range of solutions in establishing grammars: to put it another way, if one wants to determine the internal structure of a generative device of considerable power, it is likely to be more helpful to find what the device cannot do than what it can.

But the drive toward universality (and reactions toward its excesses) has extended beyond the standard theory of *Aspects,* and it has led to conflict and reformulation, particularly in controversy between generative semantics and interpretive semantics.

The general thrust of the generative-semanticist proposal for improving transformational grammar is very simple: if some semantic features of sentences can be specified in their syntactical deep structure why can not all such features be specified? Why split the syntactic and semantic components at all? Why not equate ultimate syntactic deep structure with semantic representation? Or, more speculatively, one can ask, why not take the system of semantic representation to be something like the familiar predicate logic (with perhaps a few additions), and the base to be such a system supplemented with a relatively small number of "atomic predicates," or semantic primitives, universal to human thought? The words of particular languages, just as their surface syntactical structures, would decompose into extremely abstract and complex syntactic-semantical deep structures; the features constituting the lexical-syntactical peculiarities of a language would be given as a series of transformations relating the syntactic-semantical deep structures (or "natural logic formulas") of the "universal base" to their particular realizations in the language in question, similarly for the peculiarities of other human languages.

For example, instead of relating *women are murdered by men* to an *Aspects*-type deep structure along the lines of (*men* ((*murder*) (*women*)))   which will
NP   Verb   NP VP Sentence
serve as input to the semantic component, a generative semanticist will suppose that the ultimate syntactical deep structure will be, minus some complicated bracketing, something like *cause to become not alive—men—women* (where *cause to become not alive* is to be understood, not as English, but as the lexical decomposition of the English lexeme "murder" into the nonterminal semantic primitives, or atomic predicates, that are universal to human thought). For another example, the generative semanticist argues that just as an *Aspects*-type syntax can explain *the fighting stopped* to be generated from a deep structure in which the logical subject (those who fight) appears, so it ought to be amended to explain that *John received a letter* derives, ultimately, from a syntactic-semantical deep structure more on the lines of *someone sent John a letter*, in which the "real" logical subject appears. In both cases, the step beyond *Aspects* is that syntax is not conceived of as rules specifying how the words (or *formatives*) of a particular language can be combined; rather, syntax operates first in combining universal conceptual elements into natural logic formulas (the universal base) and these formulas are transformed, by universal and specific rules, into particular sentences, composed of words peculiar, syntactically and phonologically, to the language in question.

Two other ways in which the generative semanticists have suggested extending the notion of deep structure are derived, with considerable change, from the work of the Oxford philosophers, J. L. Austin and P. F. Strawson. Austin (1962) coined the term *performatives* for utterances such as *I promise to return your book tomorrow* which are characteristically present tense, first person, with a verb that names the *speech act* actually done by the person who says the performative (in appropriate circumstances)—a case of *doing*, as opposed to saying, things with words. But Austin subsequently came to emphasize that there was a performative element (or "doing") in any utterance. To say *I state that I was there* is to do something, namely the act of *stating*. To say *I was there* is also to do something: again, the act of *stating*. Austin, who probably derived his emphasis on *doing* things with words from a similar emphasis in the leading British linguist of his generation, J. R. Firth, and who read Bloomfield with sympathy, never wrote anything to suggest that *I state that I was there* might be, as a matter of syntax, something like the deep structure of *I was there*.

Austin, though he died before the publication of *Aspects*, was notably unsympathetic to notions like deep structure found in the work of philosophers. But it is easy enough to see that since generative semanticists are in principle inclined to the view that such a linguistic, presumably semantic, phenomenon ought to appear in syntax, it would be very tempting to suppose that every declarative sentence (used in a declarative speech act) had, as a matter of syntax, a deep structure somewhat along the lines of *I say (declare, communicate, etc.) to you that* followed by the surface declarative, which is derived by some transformation that deletes the deep-structure performative element. To pass muster, of course, this performative analysis, primarily associated with Chomsky's colleague J. R. Ross, must be supported by specific syntactical arguments. Ross (1970) gives a number of arguments purporting to show that a syntax will generate the sentence of English more simply and revealingly if such deep performatives are assumed. I will not say anything about these arguments—Chomsky has expressed skepticism about them—except to say that they are similar to the much simpler argument that since syntax must generate *you suit yourself* and not *she suit herself*, etc., one can compactly explain the similar status of *suit yourself* and *suit herself*, etc. by assuming that they would derive from the deep structures underlying the longer sentences by some deletion transformation.

Strawson, in various publications, has made popular the notion that part of the logical, or semantic, analysis of sentences should consist of a specification of the *presuppositions* made by those who issue such utterances. The statement 'John's children are asleep' *presupposes* that John has children, etc., and *states* that those presupposed children are asleep. If John's children are awake, what is stated is false; if John has no children, it is not so much that the utterance is false as that it is void, odd, or whatever, through the failure of its presupposition. In Strawson's classic essay on the notion of presupposition, "On Referring" (1950), he claims that utterance of *The present king of France is bald* presupposes, rather than states, that France has a king; whereas it states, rather than presupposes, that the presupposed individual is bald. Strawson was criticizing Bertrand Russell's famous analysis, in "On Denoting" (1904), of such definite descriptions and their logical form (or what was sometimes called, long before transformational grammarians appeared, *deep grammar*). Russell, in an analysis that may remind the reader of Chomsky's analysis of *Invisible God created the visible world*, claimed that though the sentence superficially consisted of a subject, *the present king of France*, and predicate, *is bald*, its logical form was equivalent to three propositions (1) there is a (present) king of France; (2) there is no more than one king of France; and (3) he is bald. Russell maintained that, in uttering *The present king of France is bald*, one stated all three of these propositions. Strawson claimed that (1) and (2) were presupposed, and only (3) was stated.

Strawson held that presuppositions belonged to *statements* (made through the use of sentences). But the generative semanticists have applied the doctrine to sentences directly, maintaining that the full grammatical specification of a sentence should indicate its presuppositions. Among the generative semanticists, George Lakoff has been the most prominently concerned with presuppositions. He is responsible for the remarkable claim, mentioned earlier (p. 31), that (10) is ungrammatical unless, in keeping with the presupposition of the sentence, one is sympathetic to the New Left.

(10) John called Mary a Republican and then she insulted him

In principle, the generative semanticists suppose that the generative device that will generate all and only the sentences of English will provide them, through the steps in the generation of these sentences, with a specification such that one will obtain a full indication of all that such sentences could be said to mean, i.e., all their logical and semantical properties. They have purported to set about proving this supposition, as I have intimated, through grammatical analyses that seem to the unsophisticated observer to rest on extremely subtle and idiosyncratic (and theory-serving) judgments about ungrammaticality.

George Lakoff, for example, appeals to his audience to find that one of the two following sentences is obviously ungrammatical while the other is, equally obviously, grammatical:

(45) Last night I dreamed that I was Brigitte Bardot and I kissed me

(46) Last night I dreamed that I was Brigitte Bardot and I kissed myself

As one follows his appeals, respecting other sentences involving imaginary situations, to our supposedly immediate, untutored intuitions of grammaticality and ungrammaticality, most of which is equally baffling, the suspicion grows that the theory is wagging the evidence. Lakoff is inclined to accept a rather contentious, and certainly esoteric, doctrine held by some modal logicians to the effect that, when we talk about imaginary situations, or "possible worlds," it does not make sense, logically, to talk about what might happen to individuals of this world in such imagined worlds—it only makes sense, logically, to talk about what might then happen to *counterparts*, individuals who are only *very similar*, that is, to the individuals of this real world of ours. Granted *counterpart theory* and some fairly recent transformationalist views about the difference between the way in which "me" and "myself" acquire reference, Lakoff would have to conclude that one, but not the other, of these sentences is logically senseless (and could not be represented by a well-formed formula in a counterpart-theory modal logic).

Hence—one finds it terrible not to suspect something of the sort—the pressure to begin to feel that the sentence somehow sounds odd, ill-formed, or ungrammatical becomes enormous (any sentence that one says over and over again is likely to sound odd: if one's theory suggests that a fluent speaker should find certain sentences odd and ungrammatical and that the speaker's unreflective, intuitive perception that they are ungrammatical is evidence for the theory, then one will find it very difficult to resist feeling that one's own unreflective, intuitive perception—oh happy day!—*is* that they are odd and ungrammatical). For the benefit of those readers whose sense of grammaticality in English (similar to my own) does not provide an obvious, unreflective, intuitive perception that one, but not the other, of (45) and (46) is ungrammatical, I will add that (46) is the sentence that Lakoff considers ungrammatical. Most people whom I have asked to make a snap judgment on which of the two is odder, or more distant from normal English, pick (45), reversing Lakoff's judgment.

At this point, the reader may well ask—particularly considering that performative aspects, presuppositions, "reference through possible worlds," and so on, derive fairly directly from the work of philosophers and logicians (who did not think of themselves as doing syntax but rather as debating logical and philosophical issues of considerable scope and generality, which in the case of Austin and Strawson only incidentally involved the sentences of English and, in the case of the modal logicians, hardly involve such sentences at all)—whether there is any difference between a generative semanticist and the sort of philosophers, or philosophical logicians, with which this century abounds. Is there supposed to be some difference between what the philosophic logician does—what Strawson, Austin, and modal logicians like David Lewis and Saul Kripke are concerned with —and what the generative semanticist does? Or will the generative semanticists, supposedly simple scientists engaged in the task of the professional linguist of producing a generative grammar of English (and other languages), eventually produce definitive solutions to the problems of logical analysis that recent philosophic logicians have debated, and which many philosophers would consider to be the basic and crucial problems of philosophy? Perhaps I could put this question in a clearer way, if I permit myself to digress for three paragraphs in anticipation of what I will conclude in the next chapter.

Western philosophy during most of this century has merited, and embraced, the label "analytic philosophy." This familiar label is often explained by three familiar theses about philosophy. First, there is a reasonably clear distinction between analytic, conceptual, or logical questions, which are all that concern philosophers (though not philosophers exclusively), and synthetical, empirical, or factual questions, which concern scientists, historians, ordinary men, and so on. Secondly, philosophers are *not* scientists, therefore, though they may be concerned with the logical problems of the sciences and of other disciplines and ordinary life; hence, again, no fact, no empirical discovery, can ever determine the solution to any genuinely philosophic problem. Thirdly, in previous centuries, philosophers have talked as if they were scientists, concerned with factual problems of a fairly general sort: with the "metaphysical" task of giving *a very general description* of the basic contents of our universe and with the psychological job of giving a very general description of the contents of the human mind (their source, status, and causal and conceptual interrelationships, and relationships with nonpsychological phenomena). But—so this common view maintains—the work of such philosophers should (by paring off irrelevancies) now be interpreted as being essentially analytic or logical and concerned only with the logicosemantic analysis of what we say.

For example, a seventeenth-century rationalist philosopher like Descartes may ask the ("metaphysical") question whether minds and (material) bodies are fundamental constituents of the universe, or whether minds (consciousness, thought, and so on) are really to be properly and expeditiously explained as aspects of the complicated physical behavior of certain physical organisms? Or, to put it in a slightly different manner, which Descartes would find equally acceptable: are matters such that psychological studies inevitably deal in abstractions, concepts and forms of explanation which are only very distantly and indirectly related to the sort of physical phenomena (and theory) that nonpsychological studies consider? Descartes' rationalist and mentalist position, of course, is that minds are basic constituents of the universe and that their study has to deal in matters that are only distantly related to observed physical, and nonpsychological, phenomena. Recent analytic philosophers have felt that Descartes may be properly represented as really raising essentially analytic, or logical questions. Gilbert Ryle, in disputing Descartes' mentalism, in effect argues that Descartes' question is really the analytic, or logical question of whether our talk about "mental matters" is really to be understood as nothing more than talk about human physical behavior, posed in idioms that don't normally confuse people (excepting Cartesian philosophers), that is, involving no concepts, abstractions, or forms of explanation that essentially diverge from those of the nonpsychological sciences. But Ryle, whose antimentalist answer is affirmative, often writes as if this were just a question of the *linguistic meaning* of what we say, in English, about human beings: if we know the English language (without assuming any covert philosophic principles), we know that what we *mean*, in talk about psychological behavior, is logically (or linguistically) equivalent to talk about physical behavior.

If we accept the analytic philosopher's viewpoint sketched above, it would seem hard not to conclude that the generative semanticists will simply, in giving the syntax of English, decide the philosophic question as to whether Descartes, properly interpreted, or Ryle is right (i.e., as to whether mentalism or behaviorism is correct, or as to whether rationalism or empiricism in a broader sense is right or wrong). And, presumably, they will similarly decide all other questions of analytic philosophy. Of course, I will concede that it is possible for linguists to provide partial characterizations of the logicosemantic features of languages and discourse, just as it is possible in composition and introductory logic courses to give nonphilosophic (or philosophically uncontentious) characterizations of this sort. But the characteristic feature of questions of logic and meaning that concern philosophers is that they are not of this sort. Rather they inevitably involve empirical suppositions about the general character of the universe and the structure of the sciences, that is they involve, as in effect they must, a resolution and refinement of the loose, adaptable, multipurposed structure of portions of natural language in accord with such theoretical suppositions.

I will say more about these questions when I deal with Chomsky's defense of philosophical rationalism more directly (it will become clear that Chomsky wishes to deny the analytic reconstruction of Descartes just sketched—his defense is of the unreconstructed "metaphysical" position taken as a set of very general empirical and scientific claims about human beings and their psychological characterization). For the moment, let me say one thing in anticipation: given that I am generalizing in a crude and somewhat selective way, it makes sense to say that *if the basic commitments commonly put forward as generative semantics and as analytic philosophy are accepted*, it is reasonable to conclude that linguists' syntactical characterizations of human languages will provide answers to all (genuine) philosophic problems. The conclusion I want to draw from this—which is, I will try to argue, both in keeping with aspects of Chomsky's thought and of much recent philosophic criticism of analytic empiricism—is that there is something wrong with the relevant portions of analytic philosophy and of generative semantics. But what I want to do now is to summarize Chomsky's current interpretive-semanticist position, and, particularly, his specific criticisms of aspects of the generative semanticists' position.

Simply considering the terms *generative semantics* and *interpretive semantics*, one gets a hint that what is at stake is the autonomy, and primary character, of syntax. Chomsky today still echoes the claim of *Syntactic Structures* that correspondences between syntax and semantics are so complicated that one will do better trying to generate, and so syntactically characterize, the sentences of natural languages (and their phonological realizations) without warping this characterization by including explanations of meaning and use. The semantic component interprets the structures generated by these components; it is dependent on them in the strong sense that it would have nothing to interpret were these components unproductive.

Indeed, in Chomsky's present view, it seems reasonable to suppose that semantic interpretation will depend not simply on syntactical deep structure (as in *Aspects*), but also on aspects of surface syntax and even on aspects of phonological structure. There is now a reaction against the pressures, noted in *Aspects*, to shape syntax to fit semantics, to construct transformations so as to preserve meaning from deep to surface structure, and to formulate the syntactical lexicon in such a way as to radically reduce the generation of senseless, or odd, sentences. *Colorless green ideas sleep furiously* is once more regarded as grammatical (though semantically anomalous); generally, those who have taken Chomsky's side in this family dispute have tried to avoid depending on judgments of ungrammaticality of a subtle, idiosyncratic, or dubious sort. The change from active to passive is once more recognized to change meaning (at least for quantificational sentences). The way is being sketched to account for aspects of performativeness, presupposition, and various related phenomena as a matter of semantic interpretation at a surface syntactical level, if not in some cases at a phonological level; it is argued, above all, that this way of dealing with language is possibly both simpler and much more revealing—and more definite and testable—than the attempt to cram all this into syntax. In "Some Recent Issues in Semantic Theory" (1970), he writes:

A central idea in much of structural linguistics was that the formal devices of language should be studied independently of their use. The earliest work in transformational-generative grammar took over a version of this thesis, as a working hypothesis. I think it has been a fruitful hypothesis. It seems that grammars contain a substructure of perfectly formal rules operating on phrase-markers in narrowly circumscribed ways. Not only are these rules independent of meaning or sound in their function, but it may also be that the choice of these devices by the language-learner (i.e., the choice of grammar on the basis of data) may be independent, to a significant extent, of conditions of meaning and use. If we could specify the extent precisely, the working hypothesis would become a true empirical hypothesis. Such an effort may be premature. It does, however, seem noteworthy that the extensive studies of meaning and use that have been undertaken in recent years have not—if the foregoing analysis is correct—given any serious indication that questions of meaning and use are involved in the functioning or choice of grammars in ways beyond those considered in the earliest speculations about these matters, say in Chomsky (1957).

(p. 57)

From the point of view of someone interested in the fate of analytic philosophy, in the version I have crudely sketched, the essential point in these extensions (or corrections) of the grammatical theory of *Aspects* is that we can no longer identify the logical properties of utterances (the basis for semantic interpretation) with any *particular* level of syntactical (or phonological) structure. Perhaps there is a "natural logic" but it cannot take

its full license from syntax. How a sentence is represented at
some phonological level, for example, stress on particular words,
can remove ambiguity or determine meaning more fully; equally,
various levels of syntactical structure feed the semantic component. Were an analytic philosopher-cum-linguist to say that a
sentence was an analytic, or logical, truth, the rejoinder might
be: at what level of grammatical structure? However, I should
add, Chomsky would still maintain that deep syntactical structure would be the most important level—*invisible God created
the visible world* would reveal its most crucial logical properties,
the three propositions of its composition, at the deep syntactical
level, whereas the sentence might be said to *presuppose* God's
invisibility and *state* his creativity only at some surface structure level.

Chomsky has said, both in the paper quoted above and in
other recent papers, that the crucial problem of present transformational-generative grammatical work is that transformational grammars are *too* powerful. There is not a sufficient number of restrictions on the construction of such grammars, and
thus such grammars are not testable against each other (though,
of course, they are selected by the evidence, over other sorts of
grammars—for example, the transformational grammars of
Aspects and *Syntactic Structures* are inadequate on the evidence,
and, of course, phrase-structure and finite-state grammars are
certainly inadequate). Many critics, who are quite convinced of
the general validity of the transformational-generative approach
to language, have made this point; it is a point on which much
work must be done. But it is wrong to think of this as a criticism
of any stage in Chomsky's development of transformational-generative grammar. Chomsky has always maintained that this was
the crucial area for work in linguistic theory. The fundamental
problem of linguistic theory is to describe the essential, as against
purely happenstance, features of natural (human) language in
as circumscribed a way as possible. In other words, to approach
explanatory adequacy by accounting for the choice of a particular grammar on the part of a human language-learner given
the data about the particular human language that he is exposed
to is to specify the software of man's language acquisition device.

The problem is not how a universal thinking machine, programmed with nothing more specific or contentious than the "universal notation" of, say, predicate logic, would determine the grammar of a particular human language, on exposure to a limited number of its sentences. Such a device, which simulates, in that it makes use of no species-specfic, "innate" principles for limiting its choice of grammars, the seventeenth-century empiricist view of man as learning essentially everything from experience, would produce countless numbers of "wrong" solutions, "wrong" meaning, "a 'solution' which a normal human language-learner would not, essentially could not, think up." For that reason, of course, Chomsky found structural linguistics wrong, and for that reason Chomsky has mantained that linguistics is a branch of psychology and part of the study of the human mind. It is also for that reason that Chomsky has found behaviorism and radical empiricism wrong, at least in their stronger forms—those forms that propose to make serious theoretical and empirical claims as opposed to essentially terminological stipulations (such as, for example, the arguments of those who define their jargon in such a way that no discovery about human beings, or anything else, *could ever* constitute the slightest evidence against behaviorism and empiricism). What *is* the problem is to discover the principles, particularly specific to man in being much narrower and circumscribed than those of a generalized calculating device, that operate in language learning and are the basis for the universal features of human language.

It is particularly clear that Chomsky thinks that this is quite a problem. He has been much more reluctant than some transformational-generative linguists in making confident claims about which features of natural languages are universal and still more as to what universal features of language acquisition give rise to this universality. Chomsky has maintained that all natural languages are transformational and have rules that operate on abstract, as opposed to explicit surface, structures; that all human languages make use of cycles of transformations working on successively more inclusive structures within sentences; and he has suggested that nouns, verbs, and adjectives are likely to prove universal deep-syntactic categories of human languages, and that at least one constraint on grammatical rules, which prohibits transformations that move material in or out of various conjunctive structures, is probably universal. But he has emphasized, particularly in his most recent papers, that the confident identification of particular universals is not possible at this point.

CHAPTER 3

Psychology, Philosophy, Politics

O F course, we have been talking about these three topics all along; for Chomskyan linguistics is above all an attempt to characterize a significant portion of human psychology (as, substantially, the study of the software of human nature), and this sort of characterization can be seen as establishing some of the claims of traditional rationalism. The view of man that results might be thought to have political significance.

In this final chapter I want to talk about what Chomsky's work may mean for psychology, philosophy, and politics; about his views of these subjects, particularly as ramifications and interpretations of his work in linguistics; about the work in these fields that is convergent with his approach; and about various criticisms and misunderstandings that have been made respecting his general rationalist view of man. Psychology, philosophy, and politics are not strange bedfellows, in Chomsky's view, and this attitude makes many people find Chomsky's work exciting and important (or infuriatingly pretentious and misguided). If anything has been characteristic of analytic philosophy, or the rather more traditional (and perhaps less subtle) empiricism, and behaviorism, that has been very common among social and psychological scientists of all sorts, it is the hardly questioned conviction that no psychological discovery, no psychological *fact*, can establish, or refute, any philosophic claim (and the reverse), and that neither can properly determine the answer to any political question (at least in Aristotle's sense of politics as the practical job of deciding, and achieving, what is good for man, within and between nation states).

In part, of course, this subconscious positivism has been a result of the increasing professionalization of knowledge: our century has seen the concentration of all theoretical scientific and intellectual activity in the university, which is divided into

135

professional departments (or unions), each zealously insisting on its independence and importance. The professional academic is institutionally pressed to believe both that the claims and suppositions of each discipline are independent of the others and that generalizations which are not professional, in that they are interdisciplinary, are not really "scientific" or "objective." But, equally, this century has been dominated by a rather skeptical empiricism (often expressed in analytic terms) that insists that the truths of reason (the logical software) are quite independent of those of (or about) human nature, and that neither sort, properly considered, can tell us what we ought to decide to do politically or morally.

Skepticism, empiricism and behaviorism, the professionalization and departmentalization of knowledge—these can seem a worthy commitment to slow, "solid," painstaking progress in detail, shorn of grandiose mysticism, "moralistic ranting," and "ideology." A familiar metaphor can be inverted aptly by those sympathetic to analytic empiricism or to straightforward behaviorism: it is that of the careful, humble "hedgehog" against the wild and dubious "fox." The understood moral is that the attempt to make general rational claims about man's condition, with psychological, philosophical, and political implications—"ideology"—is inevitably a "foxy" affair: charlatanism is the only refuge of the generalist. An obvious implication of the metaphor that is not often stressed by the radical empiricist-behaviorist is that if one hires a university faculty of hedgehogs, they will defend the status quo. At least they will defend the status quo in the sense that they will firmly maintain that no attack on it can be rational and objective: rationality and objectivity come into politics only in that the hedgehogs can tell the government (any government with any goals) the specific techniques of "behavioral reinforcement" that will achieve the goals which are themselves beyond the judgment of the poor, short-sighted hedgehog.

For that is the other, darker side of the radical empiricist's skepticism: as an organized social phenomenon it is little more than a rationalization of the economic subservience of the university to the political and economic power of the status quo; for though, from the hedgehogian point of view, he can do

research in behavioral reinforcement, and so on, for the capital-
ist-imperialists or commissar-imperialists, he in fact will do the
research that boards of trustees and governmental granting institutions find proper. Thus, though the faculty and staff of
Michigan State University who trained Diem's secret police
could equally have undertaken research and instruction helpful
to Diem's opponents, or to the American peace movement, they
would not be paid for it (or even allowed to do it at all as
American citizens). Seen in this light, the short-sighted hedgehog would seem to be—as Martin Luther once wrote of reason—
a whore: he works for whoever pays and he does not question
his employer's tastes, except as to practicality. And—strangely
enough—he is likely to call any attempt to make the university an
independent general critic of society and government, "politicization" or "ideologizing." How convenient a philosophy that
allows the hedgehog to believe that any research that might lead
to a quarrel with the basic character of the established political
and economic order is necessarily unscientific and bogus foxi-
ness! The hedgehog is very likely to be a self-satisfied hedgehog;
his philosophy teaches him that the fox—since there is no real
scientific and objective knowledge beyond what hedgehogs can
get while being dutiful and doughty hedgehogs—is really an
irresponsible rogue hedgehog, stumbling about and presumably
suffering from psychiatric problems and an inflated ego, while
pretending to see truths beyond the resolution of vision proper
to hedgehogs.

Some commentators, noting Chomsky's criticism of the hedgehogian social scientist's Vietnam role, have claimed that his
attack on them is simply one of claiming that they are pseudo-
scientists, muddled by the intoxicating, dehumanized jargon of
behaviorism; and that, hence, we have nothing better to go on
than our common-sense moral judgments (which, of course, in
Chomsky's case go against United States policy). But this
seems a wrong way of putting matters, and I am sure it would
seem wrong to Chomsky. That the United States Vietnam activity has been wrong and immoral in various respects is not a
"common sense moral judgment" (that some future social science—with better jargon and so on—would replace with a genuine scientific judgment); it is simply that such activity has

been wrong and immoral—a truth on the same level with the truth that there was a disastrous world economic depression in the 1930's (or any similar obvious generalization). Chomsky has not been concerned primarily to dispute specific judgments, made by administration-employed social scientists, that one or another specific policy would have a given effect (though he has poked fun at the continual inaccuracy of such judgments); rather, he has disputed their hedgehogian claim that nothing rational can be said about the general character of United States policy—that all that could be said, by a good hedgehog, is that some specific policy could, or could not, be implemented through use of various behavioral techniques. As Chomsky has often, and rightly, remarked, the saddest after effect of the Vietnamese experience among many social scientists, apologists, former administrators, and many ordinary Americans has been that they now criticize American policy as having been ineffective: if it had worked, even if that had meant much more of what happened at My Lai, then it would have been right.

Thus, while hedgehogian skepticism, empiricism and behaviorism, and the bureaucratization of human knowledge can seem worthy humility if one abstracts human knowledge from any political or economic role in human affairs, it otherwise becomes a well-paid reinforcer of ruling political and economic forces. Of course the hedgehog may claim that he is right, that nothing but absolute moral and political skepticism is possible for a rational man. But he must claim at least that much; he cannot adopt the humble but dogged position that such knowledge will eventually come through further research. The hedgehog cannot tenably maintain that his skepticism is temporary. His claim cannot be that we may eventually be able to say, as rational men and scientists, that some portion of United States Vietnamese policy has been moral, or immoral; rather, his claim is that such judgments can never be rational and scientific. The implications of this sort of absolute moral-political skepticism (which appears in analytic philosophy as the denial of "naturalism" in ethics) are frightening both for the future of universities (as to what may be regarded as "genuine scientific research") and, still more importantly, for the future of mankind. Of course, this does not in the least prove that this hedgehogian skepticism is false; what it does show is that it is the counsel not of caution but of resignation and dispair, respecting the scope of reason in human affairs.

Chomsky sees both the possibility of a larger scope for reason in human affairs and the possibility of deriving more adequate political views from a more adequate, more rationalist, and more empirically justified view of human nature. I shall explain what I can of his train of thought in the following way. Respecting psychology, I shall first consider some criticisms that are routinely made of the notion that Chomsky's sort of work can contribute, in any important way, to psychology; providing replies to these objections will be a good way of sketching what a mentalistic psychology, in Chomsky's sense, will look like. It will also be as well to take the reverse of the coin—Chomsky's specific criticisms of behaviorism. And I want to say also a little about work, other than in linguistics, that belongs to a mentalistic psychology, or, more generally, to a rationalist view of man. Respecting philosophy, I am going to try to explain Chomsky's defense of rationalism and his claim that his work confirms Cartesian rationalism, and I want to correct what I consider to be misunderstandings of his views about rationalism. I shall also try to make sense of Chomsky's criticism of traditional and analytic empiricism. I mean in this part of my discussion to interject two views of my own: (1) that recent developments in logical theory dovetail with Chomsky's work and (2) that the notion of the relationship between grammar and language, and analytic philosophy and logic, which some generative semanticists (and by the philosopher, J. J. Katz) seem to hold is by the same token misguided. Finally, I shall conclude the chapter not so much with a specific review of Chomsky's analyses of Vietnamese matters as with a sketch of the political implications of the rationalist psychology and philosophy that Chomsky espouses.

All this will be inevitably little more than a summary review of some general points—an overview of an overview. But if one point is kept in mind, this procedure will seem more appropriate. I shall repeat what I wrote in the Introduction: one only really understands the generalizations if one sees them as labels for results obtained in the technical apparatus; until one has some

grasp of the specifics of Chomsky's work one does not really
know what he means by rationalism, universal grammar, innate
ideas, or mentalism.

I Psychology: Being Realistic About the Software

One feature that has remained fairly constant in the conflict,
respecting psychology, between empiricists and rationalists is
the choice of comparisons for man's cognitive activities. Empiricists like animals, and rationalists like formal systems (software thinking devices).

Both the eighteenth-century empiricist philosopher, David
Hume, and the twentieth-century behaviorist psychologist, B. F.
Skinner, tend to compare man's cognitive activity to that found
in animals (pigeons and rats figure in Skinner's work): the
same simple principles of learning, or conditioning, operate in
both animals and man. The tradition to which both men belong
has tended to try to explain both human and animal cognitive
activity in terms that suppose little or nothing in the way of
software. Hume's picture of human psychology is really not
unlike that of the modern behaviorist. The inputs to the mind
are various sensory stimuli—"retinal irradiations," vibrations in
the fluid of the ear, and so on. To some such stimuli there are
unconditioned responses; and continued conjunctions of stimuli
("reinforcement," positive or negative) can build associations
between stimuli and the stored memory of stimuli, thus producing conditioned responses, in other words what passes for
learning, training, adapting, and so on. Hume, of course, is
thinking about this from an introspective point of view: he is
thinking about himself thinking, whereas the modern behaviorist
is describing how the human beings he studies behave.

But the two points of view come to the same thing in that both
strive to show that cognitive behavior is nothing more complicated (in effect) than that found, i.e., concretely realized, in
a finite-state device making use of nothing but terminal symbols
(software paths, so one might mix metaphors, grooved on the
"blank tablet" of the mind by sequences of stimuli). Terminal
symbol, here, means what is, or can be, experienced as sensory
stimuli as opposed to the abstract ideas that rationalists suppose

are essential to human thought and that Chomsky has shown are essential to basic linguistic competence. Nothing goes on in the Humean mind that would make a behaviorist blush. There is nothing in it but sensory stimuli, memories of such, and associations between these, established by the conditioning of experience.

It is important to note that the behaviorist, or traditional empiricist, is tacitly supposing the existence of mental software, only it is the most simple and rudimentary of software, for man, like the animals, is a thinking device of the most elementary and generalized sort. Thus, both Skinner and Hume suppose that associations—the pathways of a finite-state device as it were— are built up between kinds of stimuli, though neither psychologist (certainly not Skinner) would suppose that they have any idea of the actual brain physiology involved, that is, the physical and chemical hardware in which these software associations are actually realized. Skinner has no way of knowing what goes on —physically and chemically—in the brains of pigeons, rats, or men, when they are conditioned to respond in various ways; the state of being conditioned in some specific way or another is a software notion for that very reason. But it is very limited and inferior software.

Chomsky's criticism of behaviorism, in his extraordinarily detailed and acid reviews (1959, 1971) of Skinner's *Verbal Behavior* and *Beyond Freedom and Dignity*, has been that when Skinner's theories, deriving from his painstaking experiments in conditioning rats and pigeons, are literally interpreted, they are clearly inapplicable to most human behavior, and trivial in genuine applications, whereas such theories—given a loose, metaphorical expansion—provide a more impoverished, and in no way more scientific, way of talking about human beings than is available in ordinary speech. Thus, if one takes a food pellet as a "positive reinforcer" and provides lever depressing (at various levels of complexity) as "operant behavior," one can get some substantial notion of how rats may be conditioned by their environment (part of Skinner's argument is that animals are conditioned by their environment willy-nilly, whether this is done in a planned or deliberate way by an experimenter, or behavioral planner, or arises naturally and inadvertently—thus we are all, according to Skinner, "beyond freedom and dignity," whether we hide this from ourselves or hunker down with the rest of the behavioral manipulators). "Positive reinforcement" can be stretched to cover not only food, money, sex, and so on, but also intellectual explanations such as "finds grammatical," "makes sense," "is right," and so on; unless "reinforcement" is defined in specific material terms—in which case it is not seen to explain much human behavior at all—it becomes an empty cloak for the more specific and more descriptive, but in no way behavioristic, notions embedded in ordinary talk.

Metaphorical, or generalized, experimental behaviorism becomes, then, little more than the insistence that human behavior can be explained on a finite-state software pattern. And that claim is open to the simple critique that Chomsky gave it. If we take the very elementary human software capacity of generating the sentences of a particular human language (of playing the Scrabble® Sentence Game), a capacity that comes to the fore universally, with little or no explicit training, early in life, and which is a component in almost any specific cognitive activity, we then have an "infinite response" capacity that could never derive from reinforcement of specified behavior.

By the same token, the Skinnerian notion that all our behavior is essentially a response (once the "delusion of freedom" is dispelled), which amounts to a kind of statistical determinism, is shown not to apply to our linguistic software. When put to the test of generating a grammatical sentence, a human being, so far as his basic linguistic capacity goes, *has an infinite number of possible "responses" available*. Since, as has been made clear, this means that no significant probability of occurrence can be assigned to the production of grammatical sentences, as opposed to ungrammatical sentences; and since (given the broad generalization that there are an infinite number of sentences in any natural language and hence an infinite number of sentences that have not previously been said) what is produced is likely to be entirely new behavior; it follows that such behavior cannot be understood as a response, or something "learned" through "reinforcement" at all. Producing a grammatical sentence is not a deterministic activity at all, and in so far as we internalize transformational-generative software, we are in that respect—at that level of psychological analysis—free beings. I must emphasize the qualification "at that level of psychological analysis," and there are three main reasons for doing so:

1. Skinner really is not *interested* in grammaticality. He is inclined to say that we produce grammatical sentences by some sort of (unspecified) "analogy" to the grammatical sentences we've previously met. But Chomsky has emphasized that this is not another sort of explanation, though sketchy; it is simply no explanation at all, a refusal to treat each sentence, of the infinite number of sentences belonging to a human language, as a distinguishable kind of potential behavior (thus requiring something far beyond finite-state software for the generation of the potentially infinite behavioral repertoire in question). Skinner has no interest in specifying the psychological software required for an infinite generative capacity of this sort; in a real sense it is outside the scope of behavior as a behaviorist such as Skinner understands the notion of behavior. His notion of behavior is of *classes* of activity (*actions*, that is, realized with irrelevant minor variations) that are frequently repeated and reinforced: the generation of an individual grammatical sentence, which, as is so often the case, has never before occurred and will never be repeated, is simply not an individuated piece of behavior in Skinner's sense. And the only way to make it such an individuated piece of behavior is by introducing the powerful and abstract software that the behaviorist rules out of his notion of proper psychological explanation.

2. At the level of brain physiology, neurology, and chemistry, deterministic explanations may very well be possible. This is a crucial point. No computer (or man) even can go so far as to literally count out the natural numbers, which is certainly a most elementary act, requiring nothing more than the simplest of finite-state software—possibly realized in very simple electric circuit, or neurological, hardware—and the same is true for elementary arithmetical operations. One can look at an adding machine as a complicated piece of physical matter, absolutely ignoring the computative software that the machine internalizes, and one might then describe what the machine does in deterministic physical terms, simply as hardware—not that we are in a position to do anything remotely like this for the human

brain, nor could we be said to understand, or know how to employ, a computer (ours or a Martian's) that we examined entirely in terms of physical hardware. An interesting reverse indeterminism might be said to occur here in that, from a software viewpoint, there would be entirely determinate solutions as to what the device should print out, in performing various operations; while, from a hardware viewpoint, it might be somewhat indeterminate what the device would actually do—given the faults that transistor circuitry, metal gears, or flesh are heir to—if given an extremely long calculation. Software may be realized in a variety of physical types of hardware (as more abstract types of software may themselves be realized in more specific types of software); but, equally, there is a sense in which most interesting software devices (any involving infinite generative, or computative, capacities) are simply beyond complete realization in hardware terms (and hence beyond whatever physical determinism may, or may not, belong to the universe). Viewed in this way, the question "Does a computer think?" is essentially the same question as "Does a human being think?" Indeed, it is only through software automata theory, through attempts to build and understand thinking devices, that man is beginning to understand what his own thinking may involve, that is, beginning to understand what sorts of software capacities he internalizes.

Oscar Wilde's paradox, "Nature imitates Art" reflects this truth: man comes to understand his own nature, as a thinking being, through externalizations of thought—pictures, writing, argument, logic, mathematics, computer theory and technology, and so on. To a large degree man came to understand the physiology of his body, not through studying animals, but through comparing aspects of his body to manufactured devices that he found familiar and explicable—how much more likely that this approach would be successful with man's unique mental capacities.

3. Both points—that the phenomena of grammaticality, and related infinitistic cognitive capacities, are beyond what a strict behaviorist might consider behavior, and that physical determinism cannot in a sense be ruled out—may suggest an even more general point. What is at stake, in part, is the question of what

we regard as man's more significant characteristics and which of such characteristics we regard as more open to study. These questions may come to involve historical and political issues. One can insist on taking the issue between the mentalists and behaviorists as a knockdown logical issue, one which ought to be solved by some decisive feat of logical analysis (certainly the devastating and unexpected failure, early in this century, of the attempt to reduce mathematics to logic, and by this reduction eliminating "rationalist software" from the universe, might be thought a knockdown for a fairly strong form of empiricism—but empiricists have gone about their business, containing and ignoring this defeat). But this approach seems doubtfully narrow. It is truer to the nature of the debate, and more productive and more interesting, to take the issue as a diffuse, multifaceted one, involving issues of fact, and spurring and directing research.

Chomsky himself has suggested that one reason that empiricism (and from it, behaviorism) has come to be regarded as unquestionable by many scientists and philosophers is that they look back to a seventeenth and eighteenth century in which a tremendous battle was fought between the forces of religion and superstition, and scientific naturalism. Though rationalists were often persecuted by the church (and Descartes' writings were declared heretical), there were many reasons for empiricism to be taken to form a natural philosophical background for the defense of scientific naturalism. This was true even though the great scientists of the period often held some rationalist views, and a much more substantial contribution to science was made by the major rationalist philosophers than by the major empiricist philosophers. Science needed to free itself from religion and from its "self-evident" claims about man and the universe, particularly about man's cognitive and moral qualities. Science needed the license to study man without presumptions: hence resulted the emphasis on the diversity and variety of human behavior (its malleability) and the search for animal analogies so far as more enduring traits might be concerned. A compromise was finally arrived at, one which more or less followed the lead of the great materialist Thomas Hobbes, who defined natural philosophy (that is, science) in such a way that God was conveniently put outside its domain. The compromise—a matter more of social history than of intellectual argument—was that scientific naturalism was explicated by empiricists in such a way that it could not conflict with, nor be called upon to decide among, the doctrines of religionists about God and about the aspects of man that were crucial for religionists—man's "higher nature," or mind and reason.

But, leaving aside this particular stretch of history, there is no reason to see empiricism as the natural fount of scientific naturalism and liberal political progress. Since the nineteenth century, much of the work of physicists (and latterly even mathematical logicians) has been a grave embarrassment to empiricists. There have been frequent attempts to explain why such work seems so alien and so dubious from a radical empiricist viewpoint; and there have been attempts at "reconstructing" such work to purge it of realist and rationalist elements. Equally, the empiricist assumption that man has practically no (innate) psychological nature, nor any built-in rationality, worked well when the problem was that of freeing science (and politics and economics) from bizarre religious presuppositions about man's intellectual and moral nature. But empiricists today, in their skepticism about talk of man's psychological nature, their championing of cultural relativism, and their belief in the endless malleability of man, may come to buttress the status quo. The way in which recent behaviorists have regarded man has taken its cast, naturally enough, from the way that they have regarded rats; the emphasis can hardly be on anything other than control and manipulation. Whatever one may think of the behavioral therapists—who are likely to "cure" homosexuality by administering electric shocks while projecting pictures of nude men—one would be reluctant to label them liberal or progressive. The war in Vietnam, for that matter, can be seen as a massive confrontation between behaviorist forces who assumed that the "winning of minds" would be a natural by-product of powerful behavioral manipulation (turning the electric shocks up a bit, the obliteration of the countryside, endless application of physical resources), and software enthusiasts who assumed that victory would follow their appeal to the intellectual and moral faculties of the people.

What these historical associations show is a simple moral. It is perhaps better to have no purported science of psychology than to have one that is fundamentally distorted by religious and social dogma—it is better to have the empiricist compromise of ruling the mind out of science than to have a false science of mind. But it would be better still to have an uncompromised and undistorted science of the mind, particularly because recent work with automata theory, or practical experience in making thinking devices, has given such work a clearer and more cogent basis, and because traditional dogmas about the mind, and the forces that support them, simply do not have the power they once did.

For those three reasons, among others, the debate between the behaviorist and the mentalist is by no means a matter of one definite logical issue. Both have something to say about human psychology. Each insists that what the other has to say is trivial, largely mistaken when viewed from a proper perspective, and bogusly inflated through fuzzy metaphors. Behaviorism and mentalism can thus be understood as engaged in a kind of competition, though one in which there is no comprehensive agreement as to what counts toward winning. Mentalism has seen a resurgence, particularly in the United States, after several decades of confident behaviorism. Considering the trivialities and failures of these several decades of well-financed behavioristic psychological research, and considering the arguments of Chomsky and others, one might simply judge that behaviorism has been proved wrong.

Certainly, a strict (or logical) behaviorist has to maintain that mentalism is wholly bogus, that what the mentalist purports to study does not exist. Hence, for such a behaviorist to admit that there *is* a competition—that each side can give genuine information about human psychology, competing against the evidence to see which will give deeper, more revealing, more comprehensive, and more testable theories about human psychology—is to admit that behaviorism is mistaken. The mentalist can be said to have this advantage over the strict behaviorist: he does not have to prove that the work the behaviorist produces is wholly false and nonsensical. All he has to do is to establish that his own work is legitimate: not necessarily show that, on balance, behaviorist work is trivial and unimpressive. But I think that this way of winning a place for mentalism is less interesting than conceiving the two schools as genuine competitors. However, I think that a disinterested observer would judge that the decades of behaviorist work have not been very productive; in fact many people have commented on the massive trivialities of behavioral psychology without having the slightest notion of any alternative. It would seem proper to give the mentalist approach the same sort of test.

This way of looking at the issue is terribly disappointing from a logical point of view (from the point of view of analytic philosophy). The desire, as I have remarked, is to find a knock-down argument either for behaviorism and empiricism or mentalism and rationalism. Indeed, there are several available, going one way or the other, and they all merit attention. But the alternative way of looking at matters has three obvious points in its favor: (1) it has a measure of historical felicity in that purely logical demonstrations have not decided the issue and presumably will not. (2) it has a measure of methodological justification in that it encourages both sides to show that they can provide cogent, revealing, and testable theories about human psychology, rather than resting content with purely logical justifications; and (3) it emphasizes that the issue is, in good measure, empirical. Since I think we now know next to nothing about the human mind, and since I believe that we can learn a great deal about it, this last point seems very much in order. After several decades during which analytic philosophers have taken it for granted that philosophy is concerned with logical issues to whose solution no discovery of empirical science can make the slightest contribution, one finds this point, and prospect, refreshing.

To move from this general debate to some particular questions that have been raised about the relationship between Chomsky's work and psychology, I am going to comment briefly on six questions:

1. *How can it make sense to say that we "internalize," or "know," the rules of English grammar, even though this knowledge is not available at the level of conscious thought?* This question was one that has disturbed many philosophers, and

certainly disturbed me, in reading Chomsky. Chomsky again and again insists that ordinary speakers of English "internalize," or "know," the transformational-generative rules of English, even though, as Chomsky freely admits, we are not conscious, and very likely cannot become conscious, of these rules. (Chomsky, I might interject, also admits that he makes a reasonably clear departure from traditional rationalism on this point.) Philosophers have tended to think of knowledge as a matter of conscious thought alone, and most analytic philosophers have been extremely skeptical of the very notion of "unconscious thought." Consequently, they have suggested that the conflict between behaviorism and mentalism was really over the question of whether (conscious) thought can be scientifically studied.

One of the most startling aspects of Chomsky's thought is his departure from this viewpoint. He in a sense agrees with a philosophical behaviorist, like Ryle, in thinking that the difference between our mental and physical abilities is not that the first requires the accompaniment of conscious thought, but rather that mental, or cognitive, abilities are dispositions to exhibit correct answers to certain kinds of tasks—cognitive tasks: the difference is not whether one's physical activities are duplicated by plunking on the keyboard of the imagination or not, rather it is whether speaking, or writing, successfully exhibits cognitive traits. As Wittgenstein similarly remarked, we can say that a man is doing arithmetic, or thinking, if the proper symbols appear on his writing pad in the proper way, even though there is no suggestion that these symbols are appearing in his mind's eye, as an image in his conscious thought. The twist Chomsky gives to the argument is this: mind is the software of human psychology, and thought is individuated as instances of the mind's operations. The behaviorist is seen to be insisting—in the theoretical framework suggested in the vocabulary of "reinforcement," "response," and so on—on a very minimal sort of software; the rationalist is out to show that much more powerful and abstract, perhaps in good measure innate, software has to be involved.

One can feel unhappy with Chomsky's particular way of putting, or productively narrowing, the issue, but it is not an unreasonable viewpoint. Chomsky has an interesting and important

sense of *know* at hand. He is looking at men in a way that has
an established and well-defined sense when applied to thinking
devices. We do make sense of the claim that a machine which
is adequate to do arithmetic—in terms of outputs given to inputs—must have software of a certain power. When one says of
a person, or a machine, that he "knows" arithmetic (or "internalizes" its principles), one may have in mind this sort of truth.
The question is whether and how it is possible to give a circumscribed specification of what sort of software the human thinking device must have to "solve" the input of limited samples
from any particlual human language, and of what particular
sorts of solutions, within the limits set by innate human-language-acquisition software, the human mind produces.

The critic worries about the way Chomsky extends the cognitive vocabulary of conscious thought—"solve," "derive," "hy-
pothesize," "know"—to largely unconscious processes and the
way he compares the child exposed to various linguistic samples
to the linguist with his corpus. But this extension has been
found natural and useful in talking about thinking machines
(or marks on the paper of logical or mathematical texts) insofar
as they have certain software characteristics. And, to give credit
due, the philosophical behaviorists have convincingly argued
that "consciousness" as "images in the mind" does not really
explain much about cognitive activity. Consequently, it is hard
to rule out Chomsky's extension of our cognitive vocabulary.
Experimental psychologists working with visual perception—
and with some of our other senses—have also found this kind
of extension very natural and useful.

2. *Why not aim for a "performance model" in linguistics,
rather than a competence model such as Chomsky proposes,
which is neutral between speaker and hearer?* One has a tolerably clear notion of what Chomsky means by a competence
model—a grammar of a language—and so a fairly clear notion
of what linguistic competence is supposed to comprise. But this
model is neutral between speaker and hearer and represents a
considerable degree of abstraction from the actual temporal
sequences of operations that are involved in speech activity. For
this reason it is sometimes suggested that a performance model
would be closer to being a realistic psychological model. If,

as Chomsky has convincingly argued, linguistics is a branch
of psychology, why not aim for something closer to the actual
psychological processes involved?

When performance is contrasted with competence, at least
three notions may be involved: (1) one might have in mind
literal incidents of performance, the peculiarities and irregularities of the sounds as produced, or heard, as part of the psychophysiological history of individuals; (2) one might have in mind
a model (an abstract simulation) of linguistic performance, a
model that would specify the operations involved in identifying
a sentence from auditory clues, and the operations involved in
moving from a "thought" (whatever that would amount to in
this context) to the production of a particular phonological
structure; and (3) one might have in mind a model of general
cognitive performance that would add to (2) various cognitive
capacities and operations that contribute in various ways to
the cognitive performance within which purely linguistic capacities function. It is not often clear, when people suggest that
performance grammars are more realistic than competence
grammars, whether they mean (2) or (3), or how they can distinguish (2) and (3). Clearly all human beings have general
cognitive abilities that are not purely linguistic: the ability to
use inductive and deductive reasoning to perform minimal
sorts of mathematical operations, to put together sensory clues
into perceptions, to store and tap various sorts of information,
and so on. It is difficult to doubt that these general abilities
figure in various ways in normal speech and hearing. Hence, a
complete and realistic performance model would seem more
like (3) and would seem to be a general model of man as a
cognitive, not simply linguistic, being. But this model would,
for its very generality and comprehensiveness, obviously not
be a grammar, or a linguistic model, but rather something to
which the linguist would make some contribution, along with
scientists concerned with other components or aspects of the
model. On the other hand, if one has in mind the narrower
notion of performance model (2), other sorts of difficulties
occur. Drawing the line between linguistic and nonlinguistic
matters is at least a reasonably clear job when one is considering

a competence grammar; but no one has shown, so far, how this is possible for a performance grammar.

These are vague comments, however. I think an example may make the issue a little clearer. Suppose one had a machine that would endlessly produce mathematical equations; such a device can be simply and elegantly described by giving a very small number of arithmetic laws, which would generate, or specify, the same body of formulas as the machine. One can imagine a number of machines which would internalize the knowledge of arithmetic that the laws, or body of equations, specify. For example, one can imagine a machine that would tolerate considerable variety in its printed inputs (of two numbers and an operation sign), perhaps with a complex "guessing technique" for doubtful shapes, and yet come out with the correct answer; or a machine which would translate logical formulas into their representations as numerical equations, eliminating all false equations; or, for that matter, machines which would just perform certain arithmetic operations, rejecting others. The first two machines could be said to have more than the bare knowledge of arithmetic in their software; the latter varieties, less. But what seems clear is that the underlying notion is the laws of arithmetic or their realization as the body of true arithmetic equations.

Chomsky sees competence as basic in much the same way: the body of structurally described sentences that constitute the language in question, or, equivalently, its specification through a proper transformational-generative grammar. As in the mathematical example, what is essential is *what* is known; how this knowledge is made use of, in a specific sequence of performance operations, is contingent and dependent. For similar reasons, Chomsky has tended to idealize child language learning in sketching the theory of the innate language-acquisition device; like the linguist, who is seen as hypothesizing the grammar of a language from a given corpus, the child is seen as deriving the grammar of his language from the small sample to which he is exposed, rather than as working out parts of the grammar, with corrections and guesses, in step-by-step fashion. But this is not the difference between an essentially silly picture of the language-acquisition process and a more realistic one: it is the difference between an abstract theory of language learning and the interaction of various processes that would figure in a full theory of language-learning performance.

Generally, a rationalist psychology might be said to be interested in what man *is* in the sense of powers and capacities, in what he can, and cannot, think and know, not in what particular men do as a result of environmental pressures; the behaviorist *is* interested in predicting and controlling specific human behavior, in deterministic thinking simulations. One can hardly resist feeling refreshed by the thought that there might be a legitimate form of psychological research which would not be another way of figuring out how to manipulate people.

3. *What does competence have to do with brain hardware anyway?* Throughout this book I have stressed software as the subject matter of psychology, as mind—at least one sort of psychology and one sort of mind. In a loose way, I meant this to cover not only the competencies that might be involved but also, less abstractly, performance models and, for that matter, thought and emotion. All this was to be contrasted with the hardware, the chemical, electrical, and physical processes that underlie the software. Chomsky has professed a lack of concern with the question of whether all psychological matters will eventually be explained by physical theories. He stresses that such a day seems quite far off; and he speculates that were this to take place, it would undoubtedly involve an extension of the notion of physical explanation far beyond what we now understand by this notion. Certainly, many explanations now accepted in physics would have seemed absurd and self-contradictory to a nineteenth-century physicist. For the foreseeable future, the gulf between psychological and physical explanation is likely to persist; what must be defended is the legitimacy of psychological investigation. I have used the words *software* and *hardware* to emphasize that the distinction, in forms of explanation and levels of description, exists in our talk about computers, though both the hardware and software of such thinking devices is much less complicated and much better understood. The point is to divert the misleading suspicion that what one is trying to do is to smuggle the supernatural immortal soul of religious revelation into science.

What I think must be stressed is the degree to which psychological theories and explanations tend to be freighted with analogies to physical explanations; we often fail to realize just how different psychological explanations must be from certain familiar forms of physical explanation.

We are quite used to mechanical explanations which explain how a device operates by giving a picture of the physical structure of its innards. The assumption is that one will understand a device if one can open it up and take a look inside: function is recognized in structure seen, so far as mechanical devices and familiar perceptual situations go. This works extremely well with devices whose innards are essentially mechanical, rather than chemical or electric. But it has also been a pervasive and persistent theme in research in physics and chemistry to attempt to visualize underlying structures, operating at a level of miniaturization beyond direct observation. This mode of explanation has had surprising success: again and again, the visualization of underlying structures—molecules, atoms, subatomic particles—has not only served to explain, and direct research, but more powerful instruments have allowed scientists to "see" what they had once only visualized. What is visualized has often turned out to look quite a bit like the functional visualization; moreover, it has been expected to look like it, and the fact that it does has usually been regarded as a very important, or even conclusive, verification of the theory with which the original, speculative visualization was burdened.

Of course, this extension of the presuppositions of our visual apparatus to a level far removed from ordinary experience has sometimes been misleading. Subatomic particles have presented shocks to scientists' visualizations. Such particles have been found to act in ways that seem impossible in terms of our habitual ways of visualizing—one finds it impossible to picture antimatter particles, or a particle that is in two places at the same time, even though theory and experiment demand these descriptions. This also happens at a macrocosmic level: there seems to be a real sense in which it is impossible to visualize the finite, unbounded universe that Einstein's theory specified.

The reason that it may be misleading to compare Chomsky's speculations about (unconscious) deep structures and the underlying realities of language with the early speculations of scientists about underlying molecular and atomic structures is that the comparison suggests that we will eventually be able to "see," with particularly powerful instruments, or whatever, what is now being hypothetically visualized. Just as scientists have, with better microscopes, come to see structures rather like the ones they originally visualized as underlying what they could then observe, so it is hard to resist the feeling that Chomskyan claims about what a competent speaker internalizes, about his unconscious knowledge of deep structure, might, or should, be verified by some sort of physical picture of the structure of brain operations—one which would confirm Chomsky's theories in that what would eventually be seen through more powerful instruments would resemble the purported underlying machinery hypothesized in the abstract software description. If one tries to put this rather general speculation into specific terms, one begins to see how misleading it might be.

To understand the human skeletal and circulatory system, man has but to take a careful look inside himself. One needs to hedge this statement by adding that man's experience with plumbing and levers helped him understand what he saw when opening the body. But still it remains true that to understand the functional aspects of these systems is to *see* their structure. This sort of possibility just does not seem to be available with brain function (that is, with mind). We have looked inside the brain, and we do know its physical, or mechanical, structure as well as we know any other part of the body. We do know that it is electrochemical "structure" that must be the basis for brain function; but we have, as with complicated electrochemical phenomena generally, very little sense of how such "structure" can be seen as a picture.

On a much simpler level, it is often remarked that our intuitive picture of electrical currents, like that of blood circulation, is that of water running through pipes; but while our intuitive visualization of blood circulation corresponds directly with what it pictures, electricity in several respects does not act like anything one can visualize as running through any sort of pipe system. One makes diagrams of electrical circuits which show functions but have no close resemblance to what actually happens; one cannot picture electrical systems as one can picture mechanical systems. Of course, this difficulty increases a thousandfold when the electrical system is much more complex, when it is miniaturized, when, instead of working through fixed mechanical components, the system operates through biochemical circuitry, when functional elements, particular memories for instance, seem present in several different physical locations in the brain.

In other words, it may be that the best sort of picture one will ever be able to give a native speaker of English, for example, *the* thought, *Charlie thinks Nixon is a national disaster*, is the "functional diagram" provided by the following thirty-seven symbols: Charlie thinks Nixon is a national disaster. And the purpose of an adequate grammar of English would be to give a more precise—more formal, explicit, and general—explanation of how to read this functional diagram. Similarly, in many cases, the best functional picture one may ever be able to give of what thought sequence occurs (consciously or unconsciously) in a human being who moves from a complicated environmental presentation to an intelligent response, may be a series of English sentences, with an appropriate linguistic and psychological gloss. (What is *not* being suggested is that these functional diagrams correspond to a conscious brain imagery, or that their correctness is eventually to be established through physiological research.)

In any case, what must be emphasized is that when one speaks of confirming, or correcting, Chomsky's picture of linguistic competence through psychological research, the research must itself be essentially psychological in that what is studied is software and what is established is functional, not observable physiological, process.

4. *What experimental confirmation has there been respecting adult and child grammatical capacities?* Speaking strictly, it is of course an experiment for a linguist to ask himself, or his next door neighbor, whether a sentence is ungrammatical or ambiguous. But what one normally means by a psychological experiment, in this context, is a ritualized laboratory procedure, where subjects are tested, in essentially repeatable ways, with reasonable attempts made to avoid bias and subjectivity. Experi-

mental work in psycholinguistics, while now largely committed to a Chomskyan view of grammar, still tends to be as careful as previous behavioristic experimental psychology in trying to avoid giving subjects very much of an idea of what is being tested and what result is expected, through fear of prejudicing subject response.

Chomsky's work has naturally suggested experiments concerning the language acquisition of children and the psychological reality of transformational rules and deep structures.

Some early experiments with adults based on the grammar of *Syntactic Structures* were influenced by the natural tendency, which I have just mentioned, to expect underlying psychological processes to manifest features in somewhat the same direct way as underlying physical mechanisms. In particular, it was thought that transformational complexity ought to be proportional to the length of time taken in recognizing (or producing) a sentence: the more optional transformations, the longer the time of recognition (or production). Experiments were run that seemed to show, with fair uniformity, that negative, passive, or question transforms of kernel sentences took a longer time to process than the kernel itself, while sentences with two optional transformations—negative *and* passive, question *and* passive, and so on—took still longer. One specific way the transformational complexity thesis was tested was by determining how long it took subjects to tell that a sentence applied to a picture, and, discounting other factors, the length of time did turn out to be proportional to the number of transformations in the sentence. Another test was that of determining how long subjects took to arrive at a sentence that had a given transformational relationship to another sentence (this test had the disadvantage that subjects first had to be taught what transformations were). The assumption underlying these tests was that a person, in understanding a sentence that he hears, first "de-transformationalizes"; and, when producing a sentence, first arrives at the underlying kernel string and then applies transformations to it—with each optional transformation (or "de-transformation") taking a specific time in the range from half a second to a second (and roughly twice that for two transformations, and so on).

Psycholinguists came to feel somewhat unhappy about these tests of the early 1960's, not so much because they were based on such an early version of transformational grammar but for three other reasons. First, subsequent tests showed deviations from these results and seemed to suggest that semantic factors were really much more important (for example, sometimes the negative transform is more familiar and natural semantically than the active). Secondly, given that the brain is obviously capable of carrying on (as is a computer) thousands, if not millions, of sequential operations within a second, and given that syntax probably involves some of the most primary and automatic of brain processes (hence, the most rapid), the assumption that syntactical operations should take grossly measurable lengths of time seems very dubious. Thirdly, the assumption that, in hearing sentences, we "de-transformationalize" them and then follow them back up the phrase-structure tree, and vice versa in speaking (and all this with the economy and elegance of derivations in grammar), seems to contradict what we know of cognitive and perceptual psychological functioning. Indeed, several more recent experiments have led to the suggestion, which Chomsky seems to favor, that performance probably involves various forward-guessing and backward-readjusting scanning techniques, that is, it involves guessing some of the rest of a sentence on the basis of the first few words, moving back to readjust first impressions on the basis of later words, and so on. Much research is being carried on in this area.

Another sort of work has been concerned with establishing the psychological reality of deep structure by showing that in many cases people unconsciously divide sentences more in accordance with divisions of their deep structure than with those of surface structure. It has been shown that if a clicking sound is made while a person is listening to a sentence, and the person is asked to indicate when the click occurred in relation to the sentence, he will tend to displace the click to a major structural division in the sentence, that is, he will think that he heard the click at such a division although in fact the click may have occurred before or after the division. If one takes sentences where major divisions in surface structure do not coincide with those in deep structure, there is some evidence that click displacement is influenced by deep-structure features that are not apparent in surface structure.

For the reader who wishes to read more about psycholinguistic experiment, I would recommend two books particularly. The first, which is introductory, and extremely clear and insightful, is a Penguin paperback, *Psycholinguistics: Chomsky and Psychology* by Judith Greene. The second, which contains state-of-the-art summaries and speculations, deriving from a 1971 summer conference, is *A Survey of Linguistic Science,* edited by W. O. Dingwall. This second book, which is very much concerned with the crucial problem of constraining the power of grammatical rules and with various more directly experimental levels of linguistic investigation, is unfortunately currently out of print; however, it should be obtainable in a good academic library. The past decade has seen hundreds of publications on the subject of child language learning, and a large proportion of the more recent work has been strongly influenced or directed by Chomsky's work, though some of it is critical of Chomsky's views about language acquisition. Much of this work has accepted Chomsky's view that one ought to understand the child as trying to construct the grammar of the language it is exposed to by trying various hypotheses, presumably on the basis of various innate principles. Considerable evidence has been gathered that suggests that children have innate development patterns; hence, they are only able to grasp certain kinds of syntactical structures at a certain level of development and it makes comparatively little difference how much exposure to the structure the child receives. On the other hand, children do not seem to learn the grammar of their native language as fully and as early as was initially thought. Bibliographical references may be found in the development section in Dingwall. Chomsky's wife, Carol Chomsky, has written a book on this subject titled *The Acquisition of Syntax in Children from 5 to 10* (MIT Press, 1969).

Respecting the sort of psycholinguistic experimentation I have mentioned, two points seem in order. First, from Chomsky's viewpoint the difference between a competence model and a performance model is not the difference between mere speculation and experimental test nor is it a matter of purely linguistic work as opposed to empirical psychology. Chomsky's claim is that both models are empirical and that the model of competence forms a central component in the model of performance. Certain aspects of the model of performance will no doubt be more directly open to test in laboratory conditions. Secondly, these various tests could not have been envisioned without the competence model provided by transformational grammar. The click test, for example, could not have been made without the reasonably well defined notion of deep structure provided by grammar. In other words, just as the notion that the only real way to start to understand the mind is through brain biochemistry and neurology gives way to the realization that an essentially psychological approach has real, independent worth—with the two converging and supplementing each other only in a very distant way for the immediate future, the psychological study more likely directing the physiological than the reverse—so competence will be specified at some level of abstraction from performance, with competence more likely to direct the study of performance than the reverse.

5. *How important are man's syntactical abilities?* Many people are prone to have a certain contempt for syntax. The ability to play our expanded version of the Scrabble® Sentence Cube Game, even with tens of thousands of words rather than the few scores available on the twenty-one cubes of the actual game, seems a trivial and useless ability. Aside from when we play such a game or while we are in elementary school, we never simply set out to speak grammatical sentences, nor, when listening, do we ever simply set out to recognize grammatical sentences. Of course, people *do* work hard to speak with polish, verve, and rhetorical force, to speak as do one sort of elite or another, to speak in an exceptionally, or ideally, logical and learned style. But what every reasonably normal native speaker does without conscious thought may seem hardly worth study.

The behaviorist psychologist, who is interested in the contingencies of behavioral reinforcement, finds a talent beyond, or beneath, his particular way of studying human beings. And, leaving behavioristic psychological research aside, those concerned with intellectual matters, when attending to words, sentences, and sentence sequences, are hardly ever, and never essentially, concerned with syntactical matters; their concern is with logical, theoretical, and (broadly speaking) semantic issues. As Chomsky pointed out in talking about the vocabulary of structural linguistics, a science, or scholarly discipline, makes the vital terms of its vocabulary theory-laden. Definitions of these terms, whether tacit or explicit, cannot be regarded either as mere stipulation *or* as a matter of ordinary usage; rather, such definitions contain, whether this is recognized or not, empirical presuppositions; they imply claims about the subject matter of the science, or discipline, which may well turn out to be false after further empirical research is undertaken.

Hence, it is a characteristic feature of discussions among such theoreticians that when they consider it important to ask whether it *makes sense* to say whether sentence A or sentence B *logically follows from* or *theoretically (analytically) must mean the same as* sentence C or whether *it is self-contradictory to maintain* that sentence A or sentence B has the same reference, or meaning, as sentence C; all such discussions involve empirical and theoretical issues and are not, except in the most superficial sense, concerned with what belongs to the grammatical competence, or to the lexical and semantic sensitivities, of the ordinary speaker of the particular natural language in which these empirical and theoretical questions are posed.

I believe it to be the height of silliness to think that when linguists debate about the definitions of "phoneme" or when physicists debated about whether it made sense to say that a photon of light was both a wave *and* a particle, and so on, that these scientists debate issues that ought to be resolved by determining what the ordinary fluent speaker of English (presuming him to be neither linguist nor physicist) means by these terms. As a matter of principle, I believe it follows that *if* the logicosemantic properties of words or sentences seem to become the focus of a serious question in the theory of some science or discipline, it will then be the case that the theoretical question in hand cannot be resolved by consulting the idealization of the competence of the native speaker of the language in question that is provided by an adequate grammar of that language.

To pick a familiar example in discussions of meaning, I think it is trivially true that *oculists are eye-doctors* and that it is true in virtue of the knowledge of English that belongs to the competent speaker of English; but when philosopher-logicians debate, as a serious theoretical question, whether it is an analytic truth or not, it follows by the very fact that this is a serious theoretical question of philosophical logic that the question is not to be resolved by consulting a linguist's characterization of what belongs to the competence of an ordinary speaker of English. Equally, the question—hotly debated between intuitionists and their opponents in logicomathematical theory—as to whether a proposition logically follows from its double negation is just not a question that can be solved by consulting an adequate grammar of English (even assuming that the examples these mathematical logicians consider are in English). Of course, when all theoretical questions are resolved, when all the relevant data is in, then one might give a grammar (of whatever language might be spoken) in which all these resolutions would be reflected—but then, of course, there obviously would be no serious theoretical questions to resolve by consulting such a grammar. To insist that theoretical questions have empirical content is to insist that such questions are not to be resolved by consulting what belongs to the linguistic competence of the ordinary speaker of the natural language in which these questions are formulated.

Chomsky's interest in syntax is an attempt to get at the formal principles that are peculiar to human psychology. If this attempt is to be successful, it must be isolated from serious questions of logical theory and from the theoretical questions of various empirical sciences and disciplines that have a logicosemantic aspect. Syntax must be distinguished from semantics. Another way to put the point is to say that when theoreticians debate whether something *makes sense, logically follows from,* and so on, they are not asking questions about human psychology (except coincidentally), that is, they are not asking what *makes sense* or *follows from* as a peculiarity of human psychology; rather, they are asking what *makes sense* or *follows from* for *any kind* of logical thinking. Hence, from such theoretical debates nothing much follows about what is peculiar to human thinking, psychology as opposed to logic, or scientific theory. Syntax thus purports to be a study of some of the most formal and pervasive features of mind peculiar to human psychology.

If one came upon a thinking device and wanted to understand the peculiarities of its software, and one knew that this thinking device was nondeterministic and likely to make entirely original outputs with great frequency, would not it be sensible just to collect every output of the machine in order to ask the question *what must be the peculiarities of the operations of a thinking machine that produces these sorts of sequences of symbols and no others?* If, so to speak, one managed to ask the machine logical questions, one might well get logical answers, but that would tell one little about what was peculiar to the psychology of the machine. As the philosopher W. V. O. Quine once put it in a somewhat different connection, when we are trying to understand (and so to translate) the radically unfamiliar language of another thinking being, we more or less have to assume that the other is logical, at least in a minimal sense.

Undoubtedly, the attempt to discover the psychology of the sort of machine in question would be furthered if one found that each would adopt a particular language only after a limited exposure to samples from a highly restricted range of languages.

6. *What would a mentalist psychology look like in areas other than linguistics?* Having grasped the basic elements in Chomsky's approach to language, one may ask how they can be generalized respecting cognitive and perceptual psychology apart from linguistics. A mentalist approach can have, and has had, a more general application. Indeed, though the rationalist philosophers emphasized man's linguistic abilities, they were as much, if not more, concerned with visual perception, stressing against the empiricists that one's ordinary perception of objects demanded active mental contributions rather than a simple passive reception of the light reflected from the objects. And it is to a strong, independent rationalist-tinged tradition in the recent study of visual perception, stemming in part from gestalt psychology, that those impressed by Chomsky's work refer (see J. A. Fodor [1968], J. J. Katz [1971]).

Man developed his first "externalization of mind" in permanent form through pictures, with the great work of abstraction, written language, flowing eventually from this. Just as written language became the first object of conscious, systematic study, rather than the spoken language, so pictures, as an object of conscious,

systematic study, could be said to have first made man aware
that visual perception could be laced with theories about what
is seen. And just as Chomsky has argued that speech cannot
be regarded, or described adequately, as neutral sound, but
rather must be regarded as laden with grammatical system, with
acquired and innate abstractions of mind, so the field of visual
perception—what we see with the "intelligent eye"—cannot be
described without indicating the very substantial contribution
made to vision by our unconscious hypotheses about the world
around us. The human being does not see as does a camera,
neutrally recording "retinal irradiations" of reflected light and
then "making interpretations." The human being does not see a
neutral picture at all but one laden with a theory, or various
theories about objects, deriving both from past experiences and
from innate principles of perception. (See T. G. R. Bower's "The
Object in the World of the Infant" for a lucid account of experiments that seem to show, against the empiricist tradition, that
infants are born with the notion that the objects they see are
endowed with solidity and permanence. The concept of sub-
stance, of the external world of objects—which the classical
empiricists had argued was a mere presumption, based on the
fallible evidence of previous experience—is innate to man, as
indeed the classical rationalist, Decartes, had argued it was,
though perhaps not in quite the same way.)

The great difficulty in studying visual perception is that of
finding the object-hypotheses with which it is structured, given
that visual perception is so natural to us that we find it difficult,
or impossible, to imagine seeing things in other ways. Psychologists of visual perception have developed a number of illusions
and visual paradoxes that help one begin to see the principles
on which our vision is based, by showing us clashes among these
principles or by showing us how completely misleading our
visual perception can be (and how subsequent experience can
suddenly cause us to see something, irreversibly, in an entirely
different way, even though we are looking at exactly the same
array of objects from exactly the same perspective).

Line drawings which can be seen in two ways are familiar
to most of us, for example, stairs which seem to come toward
one or seem to retreat. What seems to be the silhouette of a

goblet can equally appear to be a human profile, and so on. It is important to note that similar illusions can be created with three dimensional scenes. Naturally enough, this phenomenon reminds one of the structural ambiguity that Chomsky pointed out in sentences such as *Flying planes can be dangerous.* In both cases, the point is that the ambiguity reveals the clash of two hypotheses about the real, underlying structure of what is perceived. This also suggests that unambiguous perceptions are equally mentalistic, or theory-laden, but in such normal cases there is no clash of principles. By examining cases where presuppositions clash, one can come to understand what they are and how they work in normal cases.

In his *Philosophical Investigations*, Ludwig Wittgenstein spent some time talking about a figure that could be *seen as* a duck or as a rabbit. What he was taken to be stressing is that we are always *seeing things as*, that our visual perception is normally laden with views taught us by our culture and experience. But surely it is also possible that much of this is innate and that just as any normal human being will see a certain wave length of light *as* red, so any such normal human being will see a certain visual input *as* a solid object with certain characteristics. Someone who says, "I see a *red* spot" is taking no less of a step away from skepticism than someone who says, "I see a *solid* cube."

In his delightful book *The Intelligent Eye*, R. L. Gregory ingeniously illuminates the claim that visual perception is a continual series of "object-hypotheses" about the external world, built up of, and selected through, sensory experience. One sees there, as with Chomsky's work, the profitable extension of the vocabulary of highly conscious thought, of formal systems, to unconscious, or subconscious, mental activity. In ever so many cases, one clearly understands that one's visual perception is in the grip of hypotheses about the environment of which one is not consciously aware, and one appreciates that the extension of the vocabulary of conscious thought to these situations has great explanatory value. Gregory also emphasizes that neither our imagination nor our vision is quite the guide to what is physically (or logically) possible or impossible, as the classical empiricists had thought. He provides what strike me as convincing demonstrations that one can see (or imagine) situations that are physically, or even logically, impossible (in whatever sense of "see" is involved in our ordinary reports of having seen everyday events occur); and equally convincing demonstrations that our visual apparatus will not see, will not accept as possible, certain physically real situations. As he puts it, in a manner and vocabulary likely to strain the goodwill of recent empiricists, what is physically, or logically, impossible is "not given *a priori*" but must be discovered through experimental investigation.

II *Philosophy: Back to Scientific Metaphysics*

Though Chomsky's work attracted the attention of a few philosophers from the beginning, it was not until the mid-1960's that his work, and some of the claims of J. J. Katz, a philosopher colleague of his, became a topic of great importance for analytic philosophers and philosophical logicians. The general philosophic claim that Chomsky wanted to make—that recent work in generative linguistics vindicated the views of the seventeenth-century rationalists, Descartes in particular, about mind, language, and innate ideas—inevitably tended, given the recent history of philosophy, to be interpreted in an unfair, and sometimes outrageously silly, way. The extension of Chomsky's linguistics into semantic theory that Katz applied to the problems of analytic philosophy were less alien to recent philosophy and better understood, though it has generally been regarded with great—and I think deserved—skepticism.

However, though I think that Katz's attempt to solve the outstanding problems of analytic philosophy through modern linguistics is mistaken (as I have already indicated), it is a salutary mistake because it makes it more clear that analytic philosophy, at least in a certain popular rendition, also rested on a mistake, or, better, a misunderstanding of what philosophers were really doing when they did philosophical analysis. Indeed, quite apart from Katz, there has been an upheaval within philosophy that has led to dissatisfaction with the distinction between logicolinguistic and empirical investigation on which the popular construal of analytic philosophy rested, and to a dissatisfaction with the limited sort of logic, and inadequate conception of scientific theory, that went with analytic empiricism. Quite apart from Chomsky, this internal upheaval has led many philosophers into a position where they can be more sympathetic to the kind of rationalism and the kind of science of which Chomsky's work is an instance and even less sympathetic to the attempt, on Katz's part, to revive and improve the popular rendition of analytic philosophy.

The summary exposition will follow the order of the last paragraph. As with any sweeping analysis of this sort, I will generalize freely and crudely. The best I can say for this procedure is that the overview I will provide is one that brings together what a number of people have been saying these days, and saying with greater skill and respect for detail than I am, into one simple sketch. The salient characteristic of twentieth-century philosophy—analytic, or logicolinguistic philosophy—has been its detachment from empirical science. What is now proposed is the reentry of empirical science into philosophy. Another way to put this would be as follows. Philosophers have always been concerned with the most universal features of the world and with the most general theoretical claims about it: with what is theoretically necessary, or possible, rather than just with what happens to be the case in so many particular instances. Philosophers of the seventeenth and eighteenth centuries believed that such questions were to be answered through the experiments and theoretical generalizations of empirical science, that is, they believed that such answers were descriptions of the universe. This study has been called "metaphysics" (with the implication that it rests on confusion) by twentieth-century philosophers, who maintain that questions of possibility and necessity, of the philosophic crux of such "theoretical generalizations," are logicolinguistic questions and not empirical questions. What is now proposed is the return to scientific, or empirical, metaphysics.

The body of this book will have made tolerably clear, I hope, the sense in which Chomsky believes that present work in linguistics justifies some central claims of Cartesian rationalism. If one accepts the argument that human beings internalize, or know, a grammar of considerably greater power than a finite-state machine—one that essentially must make use of nonterminal symbols (that is, "ideas" [or abstract ideas], as against "images," in the philosophical vocabulary of the original rationalist-empiricist controversy)—one has accepted what is basic to Chomsky's claim to have vindicated a rationalist, and antibehaviorist, approach in psycholinguistics. I will say no more than to reiterate that Chomsky has, of course, admitted that he makes a substantial innovation in rationalism in primarily talking about unconscious mind, and the reader may judge whether this is a reasonable way of reviving a rationalist approach to mind. I think it reasonable to ask someone who would claim that this is no revival of rationalism what could be a revival of rationalism, that is, what sort of theoretical and empirical claims, in present-day psychology, would amount to a revival of rationalism? If there is no answer to this question, then I think the objection is to revivals, rather than to this particular one, or the objection is that rationalism makes no empirical claims and that seems clearly false of the Cartesian rationalists.

But something should be said about the matter of innateness. Here again I think that I have made tolerably clear what Chomsky means by the "innateness hypothesis," by "innate ideas," or "innate principles of language acquisition." Though the innateness hypothesis cannot be said to be definitely established, and, unless the central problems of constraining the power of transformational rules is solved, may be difficult to establish, I think that it is a fruitful and interesting hypothesis and well worth pursuing. Chomsky has refined and vitalized a central thread in that many things could be put under the umbrella of innate ideas in the writings of rationalist philosophers. He has stressed that the innate ideas he speaks of are not present in conscious thought—indeed he has found passages in the rationalist philosophers that suggest that they did not mean to maintain that such ideas were present in the infant's conscious mind at birth—but he goes further than these rationalists in maintaining that these innate principles of language acquisition may never be present in conscious thought.

Aside from maintaining that some principles of language and of visualization were innate, many rationalist philosophers wanted to maintain that various religious, moral, and political notions were innate—the idea of God, for instance. It is this feature of classical rationalism that Chomsky's critics have sometimes stressed, either in justifying suspicions about Chomsky's own views or in claiming that Chomsky is not really reviving rationalism. Chomsky of course makes no claim about this sort of innateness, and it surely seems silly to condemn all innateness claims because some have been wrong; many classical empiricists claimed that the existence of God, and the propriety of hideous economic exploitation, were evident empirically, but to condemn empiricism just on that basis seems equally silly. Further, I think that a review of the literature makes it clear that the issue of innateness (and abstract) ideas, as debated by the seventeenth- and eighteenth-century philosophers, was more fundamentally and more pointedly about systematic and general cognitive processes, namely, those of perception, reasoning, and language. It is this fundamental aspect of innateness, and of mentalism more generally, that Chomsky has wanted to revive. And he did it with this explicit historical reference because he found that behaviorists, in linguistics and psychology, were taking for granted, quite wrongly and with deep-seated prejudice, much the same views about human cognitive psychology that the classical empiricists had defended and the classical rationalists opposed.

What has caused a basic confusion about Chomsky's use of innateness is that innateness had come to be interpreted by philosophers subsequent to Descartes, particularly under the label *a priori*, in a special sort of way: namely, as *what is known independently of experience*, as *a built-in self-guaranteed truth*, or even, *as what is logically true*. This is not what Chomsky has in mind. He writes, for example:

> Such principles, we may speculate, are *a priori* for the species—they provide the framework for the interpretation of experience and the construction of specific forms of knowledge on the basis of experience—but are not necessary or even natural properties of all imaginable systems that might serve the functions of human language. It is for this reason that these principles are of interest for the study of the nature of the human mind.
>
> (*Problems of Knowledge and Freedom*, p. 41)

In other words, the innate principles of language acquisition have no built-in epistemological or logical guarantee, nor are they logical truths. Unless the human infant is exposed to a language that belongs to a relatively small subset of all the languages that thinking beings might successfully employ, the innate principles will lead the child either to a false solution or to no solution at all. These principles severely limit the kinds of languages that the child can learn. It is because they contain a number of such limiting presumptions about the language of exposure that they allow the comparatively rapid learning of language under less than ideal conditions. (One need only dwell on the fact that many people have great difficulty learning foreign languages, and that to speak a foreign language "like a native" is assumed to be an arduous and unusual achievement, to wonder at child language acquisition—particularly when one considers that children have no language in which they can ask questions or be told about the language that they are learning.)

The one guarantee that the innate ideas of language acquisition have is biological evolution. Languages which are naturally produced are naturally understood. Languages, or grammatical extensions and extrapolations of languages, that are easy to learn persist; if they are not easy, they tend to disappear. Conversely, children who learn languages easily and well persist; those who do not have tended to disappear from genetic history. The innate principles of human language acquisition have no guarantee of the sort that most philosophers subsequent to Descartes, and certainly those subsequent to the rationalists generally, have wanted for *a priori* truths, or innate ideas in that sense. In particular, they do not have the guarantee that Kant thought the rationalist *a priori* must require to be acceptable: that is, that they are presuppositions of cognitive experience for any thinking being. Neither do they have the guarantee that twentieth-century philosophers have generally thought the genuine *a priori* truth required, namely, a logical truth, one which would be true of, and in, any language that a thinking being might adopt. In other words, Chomsky is not interested in innate ideas as epistemologically, or logically, guaranteed answers for the philosophic skeptic who asks *what can I presuppose, and justify beyond any logical doubt, about the world around me— simply in that I am a rational being?* He is concerned with human psychology, with the essential properties that define human language and human-language-acquisition device, maintaining against the empiricist theory of learning that much more must be innate than the ability to associate memories of sensations (or, equivalently, an ability essentially the same as a finite-state device acquisition capacity).

Some have claimed that Chomsky's view of innateness differs essentially from Descartes', suggesting that "the motivation behind rationalists' postulation of an innate component ... derives from considerations concerning the *logical status* of various truths and principles which men know" (David Cooper, "Innateness Old and New," p. 482). Since recent philosophic concern with the *a priori* has concerned itself with necessary, epistemologically guaranteed, or logical truths (analytic empiricism taking these to be equivalent), there is a natural tendency to emphasize everything in the writings of seventeenth-century philosophers on innateness that fits this view. However, as Chomsky has argued, a rationalist such as Descartes would not have made the requisite distinction between "paradigmatically philosophical" questions and those of empirical science. And certainly much of what the rationalist, or the empiricist, wrote about the subject in the seventeenth century seems more like psychology, often open to straightforward experimental test, than like philosophy.

Even if one considers Descartes' most well known work, and most "paradigmatically philosophical" work (in the popular recent sense), *The Meditations*, one can see cogency in Chomsky's view. Descartes there wonders whether his innate "clear and distinct" ideas could be false, and he concludes that they might very well be false *if God were a deceiver*. It is hard to avoid concluding that Descartes is suggesting not only that a "malignant demon" might provide false innate ideas but that, if there were neither God nor demons, his innate ideas would have no necessary guarantee of truth. Indeed, the whole philosophic tradition subsequent to Descartes criticized him on precisely this point, namely, that his notion of *a priori*, or innate, ideas had no built-in logical, or epistemological, guarantee, and hence could not be called necessary truths.

But now a third sort of criticism, or comment, may be made. It may be said that Chomsky, and even in part Descartes and other seventeenth-century rationalists, are defending a kind of (methodological) "psychological innateness" or "psychological rationalism." The twentieth-century analytic philosopher—at least in the crude rendition I sketched in the last chapter—may maintain that there is a clear separation between the logico-linguistic questions of philosophy, and the empirical questions of science. In this view, philosophical empiricism, and behaviorism, are not open to empirical validation or refutation; if correct, they are correct as analytic, or logicolinguistic, truths (the assumption being that "necessary truths" or "*a priori* truths" of the "genuine" philosophic tradition are really truths of this sort). Thus, recalling the sketch of Ryle's logical behaviorism in the previous chapter, behaviorism turns out to be true on logicolinguistic grounds; the analysis of the meaning of statements purportedly about "the mind" showed them to reduce to statements about behavioral dispositions (similarly, W. V. O. Quine has more briefly defined behaviorism in such a way that it is empirically irrefutable).

One may well ask what, if one is doing "analytic philosophy," is then supposed to be the alternative to behaviorism and empiricism? That is, if one interprets (the "irrelevant") part of the debate between past empiricists and rationalists to be empirical and psychological, what is being ruled out by logical behaviorism and logical empiricism? If nothing empirical is being ruled out, which is the assumption of the common rendition of philosophical analysis, the suspicion might be that something logical is being ruled out. And I think that that suspicion is in effect surely true, though rarely put in explicit terms by analytic empiricists. In particular, most analytic empiricists have tended to suggest that all reasonable languages, and all scientific theories in such languages, could be taken to require only one, fairly minimal sort of "canonical" predicate logic, which would have no place for modal notions of *possibility* and *necessity*. In other words, the claim would be that everything empirical scientists, or ordinary men making everyday descriptions of the world around them, might state would consist of ever so many statements about what happened to be the case in particular circumstances; thus, everything that can be said consists of particular, independent factual statements, with no distinction between accidental and essential generalizations, between something just *happening to be* the case and *having to be* that way, between something just *happening not to be* the case and *having not to be* the case.

If one takes this "extensionalist" view very strictly, there is no distinction between what a competent speaker does not happen to say but possibly might say, and what he does not say and could not possibly say. Hence, Chomsky's way of describing man's grammatical capacity is logically bogus—however helpful it may be methodologically—because it speaks of what can, or cannot, be said, and on a still more general level of what can, or cannot, be learned; and this whole level of description is far from any possible formulation in terms of what happens, or does not, or in terms of statistical frequency or good guessing.

The exclusion of possibility and necessity from modern mathematical logic has bothered many philosophical logicians and analytic philosophers. Particularly, since at least the truths of logic itself (and, generally, analytic truths "true simply in virtue of the meaning assigned to their terms") would seem to be necessarily true, logic ought to make provision for logical particles that cover logical necessity. Some philosophers, who were quite skeptical about the notion that empirical scientific laws could ever be necessary, have felt that logical laws were necessary and that a logical particle standing for "necessarily" could be defined in effect as "provable in this system of logic." But, through a proof, the mathematical logician Kurt Gödel showed that this sort of procedure was objectionable; the proof was rather similar to the much more famous proof in which Gödel showed that the truths of arithmetic—the real properties of numbers—cannot be established within one logical system; hence, both proofs have been regarded as showing that both the notions of *possibility* and *necessity*, and the basic truths of mathematics, cannot be assigned meaning in terms wholly internal to a logical language, that is, they cannot be assigned truth in purely logicolinguistic terms, but depend on the reality to which the language refers.

Modal logicians today believe that the truth of claims about what is possible or necessary may very well depend on scientific discoveries, and that empirical scientific theories, or scientific laws, may very well turn out to be necessary, though not necessary by being a logical truth or by an epistemological guarantee of the sort that philosophers have thought were required subsequent to Descartes. Certainly, S. Kripke, who has been more responsible than anyone else for the recent formalization of the semantics of modal logic, thinks just that. This is a very convenient conclusion since philosophers have been bothered for a very long time by the fact that scientists have continually seemed to want to assign their theories the sort of modal character, the distinction between accidental and lawlike generalization, that could not be accommodated by the logic of the empiricist philosophers. And, of course, it dovetails with the same need of Chomsky to distinguish accidental from essential generalizations about human languages, human language, and human language learning—to speak realistically about a speaker's infinitistic powers and capacities.

Kripke offers the generalization "Heat is the motion of molecular particles" as an instance of an empirical discovery and a necessary truth (since it has neither an epistemological guarantee nor is it a self-evident, analytic, or logical truth). Equally, the statement "A human language is a transformational-generative language" might very well be thought to be a necessary generalization, though a discovery, and in no way a consciously self-evident or logical truth. (I do not mean to suggest that Chomsky has an explicit interest in formal modal logic. But he uses the terms *essential features* [of, for example, human language and mind] and *theoretical generalization* in the appropriate modular way. And he insists on realism about abstract features of the world, about what can or cannot happen, about capacities and powers.)

But there is another, and misguided, way to try to introduce the science of linguistics into recent philosophizing (though not one which Chomsky has explicitly defended, and one which he has expressed skepticism about. See Chomsky's essay in *Language and Philosophy*). That way is to assume that philosophy does consist—as in the popular, and since the early 1960's somewhat failing, rendition—of the unearthing and display of the "analytic truths of logic and ordinary language." And it is also to argue that the scientific linguistics of natural languages, particularly the semantic component, which will assign a full "logical deep structure," or semantic analysis, will be able to indicate all the analytic truths of man's natural languages. If, as some analytic philosophers have incautiously suggested, analytic truths are identified in a full linguistic characterization of the meaning of various sentences (or statements, but still within the purview of linguistic science), with such an identification in no way involving any other empirical claims, scientific theories, theoretical generalizations, and the like, then it is absolutely natural to expect the linguist to "solve all the outstanding problems of philosophy" by providing such identifications in a much more scientific, systematic, and principled way than is possible for the philosopher. Ryle, to return to my familiar example, need not have troubled about finding out whether all statements about what was going on in people's minds were analytically equivalent to statements about people's behavior. He need only have asked the linguist whether this were true. But this is doubly misguided.

It is misguided because, though analytic philosophers often talked as if they were just doing protoscientific linguistics, they in fact brought all sorts of methodological considerations and theoretical generalizations into their discussions. There are advantages that recent work in linguistics has had for philosophy: (1) the protoscientific or "armchair" phase is over, and linguists, if one accepts this silly analysis of philosophy, are prepared to do the philosopher's work for him; and there is nothing like that prospect for producing a little sobriety in analytic philosophers; and (2) in the very attempt to provide a semantics, all of the difficulties that have been said to lie in the way of this analysis, and many more, have appeared as real and practical difficulties in actual linguistics; the limitations and failures of the "standard theory" of *Aspects* could be said to reflect the fact that *analytic* is not well-defined in natural language.

But it is also misguided in a much more direct way. Philosophers have been concerned with "analyticity" in really only two sorts of ways. Philosophers have been concerned with whether there are specific instances of analyticity such that they answer some specific traditional problem of philosophy or of theoretical science, or they have been concerned with whether there "really are" analytic truths at all. As to the first sort of issue, of which Ryle's logical behaviorism might be thought a case, one need only say, as I have, that such disagreements involve in effect the theoretical vocabulary of a science, or discipline; and just as Chomsky was right in maintaining that the structuralist's definition of linguistic terms amounted to an empirical theory about human languages, so it is more generally the case that such disagreements involve matters other than the "ordinary linguistic meaning" of the vocabulary. Indeed, if these disputes were about the ordinary linguistic meaning of English words, or sentences containing them, one could only conclude that the parties to the disagreement were speaking different languages and were only deluding themselves in thinking that they were in disagreement.

But if the concern is with whether "there is really any such thing as analyticity," it is once again not a disagreement that will be solved by a straightforward linguistic characterization of English. The question that the philosopher raises about analyticity in general is similar to the question about modality, that is, a question about the character of the theoretical generalizations of science, and one which could be said to be in part about some very general, empirically discoverable features of the reality to which science addresses itself. It is not a question that is suitably approached by asking whether an adequate characterization of English-language linguistic competence will mark meaningful, or meaningless, the question "Is the sentence, 'Oculists are eye-doctors,' an analytic truth?"

Indeed, J. J. Katz (1972), after a lengthy attempt to explicate analyticity as subsumed in a scientific linguistics, seems almost to admit that he is changing the subject, for he concludes by saying that philosophy contains many, and more important, problems that do not involve analyticity. But it is an essential feature of the problem of analyticity that those philosophers who took analyticity seriously thought that *all* genuine philosophic problems were problems of analysis.

To return to the theme of this chapter: the central thrust of Chomsky's thought is to use linguistics to make a contribution to the science of the human mind, and not, save by way of general example, to provide some special trick for solving the theoretical problems of various disciplines (particularly those outside linguistics proper) through appealing to the deep logicolinguistic meaning of what is said by ordinary competent speakers of particular languages. Chomsky's concern with defending the autonomy of syntax is a reflection of this general concern; it is only because syntax is autonomous that it is possible for linguistics to make a substantial contribution to psychology. If syntax is not autonomous, if linguistics is indistinguishably entangled in all the logical and theoretical issues that are posed as problems about the meaning and logical properties of words and sentences, then linguistics will not tell us what is *peculiar and essential* to human thought, to human language function. Linguistics would then be involved in an interminable discussion of what a logical being of unlimited power and generality would think, not with the essential peculiarities of human thought, which will receive a much more constrained and specific description (if there is to be any difference between the subject matter of cognitive psychology and logic). Since man is a very adaptable sort of being, some men can make a stab at thinking in nearly any of the ways that a universal thinking machine might be programmed to think. What autonomous syntax, and the related theory of human language acquisition, might provide is some sense of what thinking operations are natural to all humans at a most basic level, not just to some under special conditions of training and adaptation.

It is a characteristic feature of twentieth-century philosophy, of analytic empiricism in particular, to hold that all philosophic problems are logicolinguistic problems concerning the logical analysis of language and that the discoveries of empirical science can *never* make a contribution to philosophy or afford evidence for or against any philosophic thesis. It is this analytic conception of philosophy that creates an apparent paradox in Chomsky's thought: Chomsky claims that the results of the *empirical* investigations of linguistic science, not on the level of the semantic analysis of particular sentences but through empirical generalizations about the psychology of human language acquisition and functioning, justify rationalism over empiricism. As one who feels that, if the discoveries of empirical science cannot in any way contribute to attempts to answer philosophic problems, this means a sterile and irresponsible philosophy and a blind and mindless sort of science, I applaud the revolt against

the analytic conception of philosophy with which Chomsky pre-
sents us. I would say this even if the serious and general qualms
I have about Chomsky's thought, aside from those few I thought
appropriate to introduce in this sort of book, should be correct.
We need experimental philosophy!

III Politics: The Nature of Free Men

As one reads through Chomsky's political pieces—mostly hur-
ried outpourings for magazines, done in time free from professional work and the ceaseless obligation of practical agitation—
one is struck by the weight of scholarship and detail, and one
can easily forgive the defects in style and the very occasional
lapses into the blurred morally dulling phrases of radical-socialist
hackwriting. In his essays on Southeast Asia, as in his pieces
on psychology, the history of Cartesian linguistics, and his surprising account of the Catalonian anarchist working-class movement of the Spanish Civil War (in the lead essay of *American
Power and the New Mandarins*), one is struck by his solid and
copious use of original sources and lack of reliance on the
standard references that most writers refer to when writing
outside their professional field (for example, the writer of this
book). The other point that strikes one is the unpretentious
moral honesty. Of course, Chomsky is a socialist and anarchist
by inclination (and who is not in some small way?) and a
Marxist in moral vision and political insight, but he holds these
positions without the slightest compromise with state socialism
or with the inflated pseudoscience, or romantic hysteria, that has
blighted much of the writing of the Left in this century.

As Chomsky would be the first to admit, most of what he
has to say about United States politics and the Southeast Asian
conflict is not original. But he has said it doggedly and he has
said it well. The strategy of my discussion is this. I will summarize—or more accurately, simply list—five central points that
Chomsky has returned to again and again, as have several others
of the Left. Then I will indicate what is new about Chomsky's
political thought, and what relates it to his work in linguistics.

One simple point that runs through all of Chomsky's writings
on Vietnam is that the United States has no *right* to tell the

people of Vietnam how to run their affairs, particularly, in that the means used to do so are quite clearly those labeled as "genocidal" and considered "war crimes" both in the United Nations charter and in the war-crimes trials that the United States and its allies held after World War II. This is a familiar indictment—indeed I think it could be said to be the common judgment of mankind by this time—but Chomsky makes the case with chilling clarity and detail.

A second, again familiar, point is that this effort was in good measure rationalized and in part directed by men who could, fairly, be labeled liberals and behaviorists. The war has revealed a poverty of moral imagination in their viewpoint, particularly in that those liberals who came in the end to condemn the war did so not because they opposed war crimes or genocide, nor because they realized that the United States has no right to tell people on the other side of the world how to live their lives, but because the methods used were not successful.

A third point, familiar at least to those who read the Left, is a critique of the "new mandarins," the academics who—adopting a lofty tone of "neutral scholarship"—argue that the problems of society are essentially managerial and can be resolved by behavioral technology armed by neutral scholarship, and that there need not, indeed cannot, be any objective criticism of the basic distribution of wealth and power within society. These same academics argue with considerable personal convenience since such a conception of neutral scholarship, and of the university, is a defense, and naturally a well-paid one, of the present distribution of political and economic power (defense of the basic status quo is neutral scholarship; whereas criticism of the basic status quo is "ideology," "politicization of the university"). Chomsky shares with the New Left an unhappiness with pseudo-scientific Marxism and with state socialism, and he condemns, as they do, the Soviet managerial elite and Soviet imperialism as much as American. However, though he went so far as to suggest carefully chosen forms of resistance to the war, he has not romanticized violence, nor does he think that there is now much chance for revolutionary change in the United States.

Chomsky has, finally, returned stubbornly to the classical socialist vision of man as a naturally creative and productive being, not a passive consumer or behavioral blank tablet, who will naturally avoid any productive effort without the goad of hunger for goods, money, or power. He hardly claims that this is more than a vision of autonomous man, as opposed to something that might be established in a future science of human nature. But he is extremely effective in poking holes in the arguments of apologists for capitalism who claim it to be an established fact of human nature that men will only work in competition for money or power, and who assume that those who are most highly paid—for example, accountants who create tax dodges for those with wealth and power—are necessarily those who contribute the most value to society.

These points are familiar and, I think, quite justified. The reader will of course think of them what he likes, though a reading of Chomsky's books will give a fresh sense of the weight that can be put behind them. The titles of the three collections make their relative emphasis clear. *American Power and the New Mandarins* is mostly about the American academic establishment as "liberal" apologists for capitalism, managerial-technologist elites generally, and United States imperialism, particularly in Vietnam. *At War with Asia* consists of contemporary reports on aspects of the war in various parts of Southeast Asia, written as a result of Chomsky's travels there, that originally appeared in the *New York Review of Books*. *For Reasons of State*, the most recent and probably the best introduction to his political thinking, is more far-ranging and contains substantial sections about politics and sociology on a theoretical level.

But only two points about these familiar themes are worth making here. The first is that there is no dependence on "scientific" Marxism, on the economic-determinist theory of man and history; indeed, what Chomsky has to say could find agreement in many quarters. The motto, which Chomsky takes as seriously as any anarchist, "From each according to his abilities, to each according to his needs," has always struck me as a natural ideal for any society; what is sometimes called the "moral dimension of Marxism" has always struck me as simply the moral dimension—for the motto is appropriate to any cooperative, or rational, society. And Chomsky's case respecting the United States Vietnamese policy rests on the largely American (Nuremberg) theory of war crimes and the Wilsonian principle of the "self-determination of peoples."

(Though Chomsky doesn't mention President Wilson, it is a fact that Ho Chi Minh, as a member of a delegation of Vietnamese, attempted to meet with Wilson at Versailles in order to ask for self-determination for people under European colonial rule. Wilson refused to meet with Ho, as he refused every other delegation of nonwhites: self-determination applied only to European whites. It was *after* this that Ho became a member of Communist parties. He tried again, when, at the end of World War II, his was the only functioning and recognized government of Vietnam; he asked for United States support against the return of the French colonial army, not wishing to depend on the Russians or the Chinese. The support was not forthcoming, and as soon as the French had returned in force they withdrew their recognition of Ho's government and began the first Indo-China War. Perhaps the greatest tragedy of recent history might have been avoided had President Roosevelt, who despised the French colonial regime and whose policy was one of supporting anticolonial resistance forces (the French ruled Indo-China under Japanese direction during most of World War II), still been alive at this point. See Bernard Fall's *The Two Vietnams* for an account of these matters from the viewpoint of a man who seemed to have found Roosevelt's anticolonialism a bizarre, and naive, prejudice, a man whose admittedly solid and carefully researched work on Vietnam has been regarded as a hallmark of liberal criticism of United States policy. I mention these matters to suggest that, leaving aside conflicts of economic policies and imperial dominions, there have been principles in past American policy that would have served this country better.)

Second, one consistent and overriding commitment in all of Chomsky's writings is to freedom: the freedom of the individual to produce and create as he will without the goad of external force, economic competition for survival, or legal and economic restraint on social, intellectual, or artistic experiment; and the freedom of ethnic and national groups to work out their own destinies without the intervention of one or another Big Brother. One thread running through a great deal of Marxist thought (as much as through the apologists of capitalism) is that the

individual, and his thought, is a product of the economic forces
at work in his environment. Chomsky, one hardly needs to add,
is very unhappy with any view of human nature that takes
human thought and action to be *essentially* controlled by environmental conditioning. Some Marxists, as many apologists of
capitalism, claim that their ideas derive from a scientific view
of human nature. The thought that tantalizes Chomsky is
whether we can eventually have a genuine science of human
nature and one, so the hope would be, which would ground
freedom, and the politics of freedom, in a scientific analysis of
human nature.

What strikes me as new and refreshing in Chomsky's thought
are (1) the insistence that politics (and so political policy)
should rest on the science of human nature and (2) the hope
that the nature involved is that of man as a thinking being,
that is, a nondeterministic and creative thinking being. This
leads to a peculiar, but explicable, paradox in Chomsky's
thought, namely, that man has the kind of free creative nature
that Chomsky believes depends on the highly constraining innateness, and derived mentalistic character, belonging to the
human mind. The paradox is resolved by recalling that it is the
infinite capacities of human thought, the infinitistic and abstract
character of man's linguistic competencies, that purport to
establish that man is by nature beyond a behaviorist or determin-
ist viewpoint. One needs a strong, built-in capacity, as it were,
before full, free creativity can manifest itself as choice within
this infinite, discrete range. A man may be free, as a rock or
an animal, in the absence of external restraint; but the freedom
Chomsky wishes to emphasize is the freedom of a being with
infinite, and reasoned, choices when so unrestrained by external
force.

Whether one agrees with Chomsky's very tentative position
or not one can hardly fail to find it refreshing in view of the
notions of politics and human nature that have been familiar
in twentieth-century political thought. One tendency has been
to suggest that man is indefinitely malleable (Skinner) and
that culture essentially determines the character of man (in
academic philosophy this view tends to surface as a denial of
"naturalism" in ethics). Another, related tendency has been

to emphasize that man is the hapless product of the forces of the market place acting on his consumer nature, or of the forces of economic determinism acting through history. A third tendency, still related I think, has been to emphasize, as behaviorism and empiricism generally, the animal analogy.

Appeals to anthropological research are used to argue that man is by nature an aggressive killer, a weapon-making and territory-claiming animal; equally, other comparisons with more peaceful animal behavior are stressed. Anthropologists can always dig up tribe after tribe that are exceptions to all such generalizations; or, for that matter, naturalists can find primates that are peaceful and cooperative, murderous and competitive, with or without social hierarchies, and so on. But all men have languages of great complexity, and any child of nature can learn the most civilized of European tongues as easily as he can learn his parent's tongue. Man is a language-using, a thinking, being—that is what sets him off from the rest of nature. It is hard not to hope that a better politics, a better analysis of man and society, could be based on such a view of human nature. At any rate, it is a view of man that should be held to with great tenacity, for it is the hope that free men, in a free society, can rationally create the good life for man.

Afterword

What has characterized philosophy in this century is a skepticism about the place of *reason*, which is to say philosophy, in science as well as in moral or political action. Equally, this skepticism can be understood as a desire to shield philosophers, as "academic professionals," from seeming more popularizers and generalists for the dizzy advance of science, and from the uncomfortable role of general moral authority and statesmansage. Hence the view of philosophy as logicolinguistic analysis, whether of any possible language or of some particular language, namely, English. Chomsky's work, and that of others, calls this intellectual quietism into question by insisting that much philosophic analysis was in important respects laden with empirical claims, and mistaken empirical claims at that. I have suggested that it is reasonable to understand the philosophic issues that arise between the new rationalists and empiricists as empirical issues, which is to say that we should sharpen theoretical and philosophic issues in such ways that lines of empirical research are seen to hold out hope of solutions.

May I add, as my own judgment, that extremely serious problems are raised for the heart of Chomsky's program by the arbitrary mathematical character of current work in grammar, and, from the other direction, by worries about idiosyncratic use of intuitions about grammaticality. And I think it must be conceded that the whole basic theory will collapse if enough difficulties accrue. But just *that* is what must be meant by claiming that the theory is empirical. The same might be said of the question, raised in the introduction, of whether the current "revolution in linguistics" is a genuine, large-scale revolution in science; namely, not enough work has been done to tell.

The reader may ask the following question: considering one allows doubts about the most central and well-established area, syntax, why press political and social judgments of the most controversial sort, particularly when these derive only very loosely and partially from this base? Of course, in much of Chomsky's writing on political issues, he simply reports what he takes to be facts and adds various sorts of straightforward moral judgments. But it is equally clear, here and there, that Chomsky wishes to draw support from work in linguistics and psycholinguistics for some of his judgments and criticisms. Those who claim to be skeptical about the possibility of deriving moral and political judgments from any facts whatsoever, who see judgments about United States policy in Vietnam, for example, as inevitably subjective, regard this attempt by Chomsky as a perverted use of science. Chomsky, of course, would regard it as an attempt to increase the rationality of such judgments, that is, as an attempt to augment rationality in human affairs or at least to reach for the possibility that there are rational solutions to moral and political problems. Still, the reader may ask: why not keep after the central, tractable issues in linguistics and psycholinguistics, with the expectation that eventually, and very cautiously, one may introduce one's new data, and rationality, into human affairs?

The answer is that one can, and should, be cautious and skeptical so far as science or linguistic theory goes, but that moral and political judgments are forced upon us, and that it is better to try to make some attempt to be rational than to let one's vote be cast, or nation committed, by individuals who are neither skeptical nor rational in assessing national conduct. It is typical that the man (W. B. Yeats) who wrote of our century "the best lack all conviction while the worst are full of passionate intensity," should have held strongly, not to skepticism, but to thoroughly reactionary and antidemocratic social views.

Selected Bibliography

An excellent bibliography of Chomsky's works to 1970 can be found in J. P. B. Allen and Paul Van Buren, eds., *Chomsky: Selected Readings*. London, 1971.

PRIMARY SOURCES

1. Books

Syntactic Structures. The Hague: Mouton and Co., 1957.
Current Issues in Linguistic Theory. The Hague: Mouton and Co., 1964.
Aspects of the Theory of Syntax. Cambridge, Massachusetts: MIT Press, 1965.
Cartesian Linguistics: A Chapter in the History of Rationalist Thought. New York: Harper and Row, 1966.
Topics in the theory of Generative Grammar. The Hague, 1966. (Also available in *Current Trends in Linguistic Theory*, vol. 3 edited by T. A. Sebeok. The Hague: Mouton and Co., 1966.)
Language and Mind. New York: Harcourt, Brace & World, 1968. The three lectures that comprise this work were given as the Beckman Lectures at Berkeley in 1967; in somewhat different form as the John Locke Lectures at Oxford in 1969. An enlarged edition with three additional essays appeared in 1972.
American Power and the New Mandarins. New York, 1969.
At War with Asia. New York, 1969.
Problems of Knowledge and Freedom. New York, 1972. The Bertrand Russell Memorial Lectures, Cambridge University, 1971.
Studies on Semantics in Generative Grammar. The Hague, 1972.
For Reasons of State. New York, 1973.
Chomsky, Noam and Morris Halle. *The Sound Pattern of English.* New York: Harper and Row, 1968.

2. Published Papers

"Logical Syntax and Semantics: their Linguistic Relevance." *Language*, 31 (1955), 36–45.

"Three Models for the Description of Language." *IRE Transactions on Information Theory.* 1T–2 (1956), 113–24. Reprinted in R. D. Luce, R. Bush, and E. Galanter, eds., *Readings in Mathematical Psychology*, vol. II. New York: Wiley, 1965.

"Finite State Languages." *Information and Control*, 1 (1958), 91–112. Reprinted in R. D. Luce, R. Bush, and E. Galanter, eds., *Readings in Mathematical Psychology*, vol. II. New York: Wiley, 1963.

"On Certain Formal Properties of Grammars." *Information and Control*, 2 (1959), 137–67. Reprinted in R. D. Luce, R. Bush, and E. Galanter, eds., *Readings in Mathematical Psychology*, vol. II. New York: Wiley, 1963.

"Review of B. F. Skinner, *Verbal Behavior*." *Language* 35 (1959), 26–58. Reprinted in Fodor and Katz (1964).

"On the Notion Rule of Grammar." *Structure of Language and Its Mathematical Aspects: Proceedings 12th Symposium in Applied Mathematics*. Providence, Rhode Island, 1961, pp. 6–24. Reprinted in Fodor and Katz (1964).

"A Transformational Approach to Syntax." *Proceedings of the 1958 Conference on Problems of Linguistic Analysis in English*, ed. by A. A. Hill. Austin, Texas, 1962, pp. 124–48. Reprinted in Fodor & Katz (1964).

"Formal Properties of Grammars," *Handbook of Mathematical Psychology*. Vol. II. New York: Wiley, 1963, 323–418.

"The Formal Nature of Language." Appendix in E. H. Lennenburg, *Biological Foundations of Language*. New York: Wiley, 1967.

"Linguistics and Philosophy." In *Language and Philosophy*. Edited by Sidney Hook. New York, 1969, pp. 51–94.

"Remarks on Nominalization." In R. A. Jacobs and P. S. Rosenbaum, eds., *Readings in English Transformational Grammar*. Waltham, Massachusetts: Ginn and Co., 1970.

Chomsky, Noam and G. A. Miller. "Finitary Models of Language Users." *Handbook of Mathematical Psychology*, vol. II. New York: Wiley, 1963, pp. 323–418.

Chomsky, Noam and Morris Halle, "Some Controversial Questions in Chronological Theory," *Journal of Linguistics*, 1.2 (1965), 97–138.

3. Unpublished Papers

"Morphophonemics of Modern Hebrew." Master's thesis, University of Pennsylvania, 1951.

"The Logical Structure of Linguistic Theory." Mimeograph, MIT Library, 1955.

"Transformation Analysis." Doctoral dissertation, University of Pennsylvania, 1955.

"Deep Structure, Surface Structure, and Semantic Interpretation." Mimeograph produced by University of Indiana Linguistics Club, 1968.

"Some Recent Issues in Semantic Theory." Mimeograph produced by University of Indiana Linguistics Club, 1970.

"Conditions on Transformations." Mimeograph produced by the University of Indiana Linguistics Club, 1971.

SECONDARY SOURCES

BLOOMFIELD, L. *Language.* Chicago, 1933.

BOWER, T. G. R. "The Object in the World of the Infant." *Scientific American,* October, 1971.

COOPER, DAVID. "Innateness Old and New." *Philosophical Review,* 1972.

DINGWALL, W. O. *A Survey of Linguistic Science.* University of Maryland Linguistics Program, September, 1971.

FALL, BERNARD. *The Two Vietnams.* New York: Praeger, 1963.

FODOR, J. A. *Psychological Explanation.* New York, 1968.

FODOR, J. A. and KATZ, J. J., eds. *The Structure of Language.* Englewood Cliffs, N.J.: Prentice-Hall, 1964. Contains the editors' "Structure of a Semantic Theory."

GÖDEL, KURT. "Eine Interpretation des Intuitionistischen Aussagenkalküls." *Ergebnisse eines Mathematischen Kolloquiums,* 4 (1933), 34–40.

GREGORY, R. L. *The Intelligent Eye.* New York: McGraw Hill, 1970.

GREENE, JUDITH. *Psycholinguistics: Chomsky and Psychology.* Harmondsworth: Penguin, 1972.

HARRIS, ZELLIG. *Methods in Structural Linguistics.* Chicago, 1951.

KATZ, J. J. *The Underlying Reality of Language and its Philosophic Import.* New York, 1971.

————. *Semantic Theory.* New York, 1972.

KRIPKE, S. "Naming and Necessity." In *Semantics of Natural Language.* Edited by D. Davidson and G. Harman. Dordrecht, Holland: D. Reidel, 1972.

LAKOFF, GEORGE. "Linguistics and Natural Logic." In *Semantics of Natural Language.*

ROSS, J. R. "On Declarative Sentences." In *Readings in English Transformational Grammar.* Edited by R. S. Jacobs and P. Rosenbaum. Waltham, Massachusetts: Ginn and Co., 1970.

RUSSELL, BERTRAND. "On Denoting." In *Logic and Knowledge*.
    Edited by R. C. Marsh. London, 1956. This article first appeared
    in *Mind*, 1905.
STRAWSON, P. F. "On Referring." *Mind*, 59 (1950), 320–344.

Index